Other Books by Max Beerbohm

THE WORKS OF MAX BEERBOHM

MORE

YET AGAIN

AND EVEN NOW

AROUND THEATRES

THE HAPPY HYPOCRITE

ZULEIKA DOBSON

SEVEN MEN

THE DREADFUL DRAGON OF HAY HILL

A CHRISTMAS GARLAND

LYTTON STRACHEY (REDE LECTURE)

CARICATURES OF TWENTY-FIVE GENTLEMEN

THE POET'S CORNER

THE SECOND CHILDHOOD OF JOHN BULL

A BOOK OF CARICATURES

FIFTY CARICATURES

A SURVEY

ROSSETTI AND HIS CIRCLE

THINGS NEW AND OLD

OBSERVATIONS

MAINLY ON THE AIR

MAINLY ON THE AIR

BY

MAX BEERBOHM

NEW YORK *ALFRED A. KNOPF* 1947

THIS IS A BORZOI BOOK,
PUBLISHED BY ALFRED A. KNOPF, INC.

FIRST AMERICAN EDITION

NOTE

I FEAR that an apology should be made to any reader of the six broadcasts that form the greater part of this book. They were composed for the ears of listeners; and though of course a writer should always write not less for the ear than for the eye of the reader, he does not, in writing for the ear only, express himself in just the way that would be his if he were writing for the eye as well. He trusts the inflexions of his voice to carry the finer shades of his meaning and of his feeling. He does not take his customary pains to make mere typography leave no barrier between his reader and him. I would therefore take the liberty of advising you to read these broadcasts aloud to yourself—or to ask some friend to read them aloud to you.

I have included in the book six other things—narrowcasts, as it were. The first of these appeared in *The Windmill,* the second and fourth in *World Review,* the third in *The Carthusian,* the fifth in *The Cornhill,* and the sixth in *The London Mercury* (and afterwards in one of the volumes of a limited edition of my writings).

The broadcasts all appeared in *The Listener;* and some portions of 'Speed' were, I am pleased to say, used by the Pedestrians' Association as a pamphlet.

M. B.

BROADCASTS

OTHER THINGS

LONDON REVISITED

(1935)

LONDON REVISITED

(Sunday evening, December 29th, 1935.)

One of the greatest of Englishmen said that the man who is tired of London is tired of life.

Well, Dr. Johnson had a way of being right. But he had a way of being wrong too—otherwise we shouldn't love him so much. And I think that a man who is tired of London may merely be tired of life *in London.* He won't, certainly, feel any such fatigue if he was born and bred in a distant county, and came to London and beheld London only when he had reached maturity. Almost all the impassioned lovers of London have spent, like Dr. Johnson, their childhood and adolescence in the country. Such was not my own fate. I was born within sound of Bow Bells. I am, in fact, a genuine Cockney (as you will already have guessed from my accent). Before I was able to speak or think my eyes must have been familiar with endless vistas of streets; countless people passing by without a glance at the dear little fellow in the perambulator; any number of cart-horses drawing carts, cab-horses drawing cabs, carriage-horses drawing carriages, through the more or less smoke-laden atmosphere. I was smoke-dried before I could reason and prattle. For me there was never the great apocalyptic moment of initiation into the fabulous metropolis. I never said, 'So this—is London!'

Years passed: I became a small boy. And I daresay I used to exclaim, 'So these are Kensington Gardens!' I liked the grass and the trees. But there were the railings that bounded them, and the pavements and thoroughfares beyond the railings. These had no magic for me. It was the country—the *real* country—the not imitation country—that I loved.

I became a young man. London was the obvious place for me to earn a living in. In my native city I abode until the year 1910, at which time I was thirty-seven years old. Then I escaped. I had known some parts of the vast affair pretty well. I wish I had appreciated their beauty more vividly while it lasted: a beauty that is gone—or all but gone. I am going to be depressing. Perhaps you had better switch me off.

London is a Cathedral town. And in my day—in the 'eighties of my boyhood and the 'nineties of my youth—London, with all her faults, seemed not wholly unlike a Cathedral town, I do assure you. There was a demure poetry about her: one could think of her as 'her': nowadays she cannot be called 'she': she is essentially 'it'. Down by the docks, along the Mile End Road, throughout the arid reaches of South Kensington, and so on, I daresay she was 'it' already; full of later-nineteenth-century utilitarianism and efficiency, throwing out harsh hints of what the twentieth century had up its horrid sleeve. But in such districts as I liked and, whenever I could, frequented, she kept the eighteenth century about her. Hampstead, upon its hill, was a little old remote village; and so was Chelsea, down yonder by the river. Mayfair and Westminster and St. James's were grand, of course, very urban, in a proudly unostentatious way. There were Victorian intrusions here and there in their architecture. But the eighteenth century still beautifully reigned over them. They were places of leisure—of *leesure,* one might almost have said in the old-fashioned way. And, very urban though they were, they were not incongruous with rusticity. St. James's Park seemed a natural appanage to St. James's Street; and the two milkmaids who milked two cows there, and sold the milk, did not seem strangely romantic. The Green Park seemed not out of keeping with the houses of Piccadilly. Nor did the Piccadilly goat strike one as more than a little odd in Piccadilly.

I don't know much about him, though I so often saw him and liked him so much. He lived in a large mews in a side-street, opposite to Gloucester House, the home of the venerable Duke of Cambridge. At about ten o'clock in the morning he would come treading forth with a delicately clumsy gait down the side-street—come very slowly, as though not quite sure there mightn't be some grass for him to nibble at between the paving-stones. Then he would pause at the corner of Piccadilly and flop down against the railings of the nearest house. He would remain there till luncheon-time and return in the early afternoon. He was a large, handsome creature, with great intelligence in his amber eyes. He never slept. He was always interested in the passing scene. I think nothing escaped him. I wish he could have written his memoirs when he finally retired. He had seen, day by day, much that was worth seeing.

He had seen a constant procession of the best-built vehicles in the world, drawn by very beautifully-bred and beautifully-groomed and beautifully-harnessed horses, and containing very ornate people. Vehicles of the most diverse kinds. High-swung barouches, with immense armorial bearings on their panels, driven by fat, white-wigged coachmen, and having powdered footmen up behind them; signorial phaetons; daring tandems; discreet little broughams, brown or yellow;

flippant high dog-carts; low but flippant Ralli-carts; very frivolous private hansoms shaming the more serious public ones. And all these vehicles went by with a cheerful briskness; there was hardly ever a block for them in the traffic. And their occupants were very visible and were looking their best. The occupants of those low-roofed machines which are so pitifully blocked nowadays all along Piccadilly may, for aught one knows, be looking their best. But they aren't on view. The student of humanity must be content to observe the pedestrians.

These, I fear, would pain my old friend the goat. He was accustomed to what was called the man-about-town—a now extinct species, a lost relic of the eighteenth century and of the days before the great Reform Bill of 1832; a leisurely personage, attired with great elaboration, on his way to one of his many clubs; not necessarily interesting in himself; but fraught with external character and point: very satisfactory to those for whom the visible world exists. From a sociological standpoint perhaps he was all wrong, and perhaps his successor—the earnest fellow in a 'trilby' and a 'burberry' and a pair of horn-rimmed spectacles, hurrying along to his job—or in quest of some job—is all right. But one does rather wish the successor looked as if he felt himself to be all right. Let him look serious by all means. But need he look so nervous? He needs must. He doesn't want to be killed, he doesn't even want to be maimed, at the next crossing. He must keep his wits about him. I advise him to dash down with me into one of the Tubes. He will be safer there, as were the early Christians in the catacombs.

They are not beautiful, these Tubes; nor are they even interesting in character, except to engineers. But are the streets above them beautiful—or interesting in character—nowadays, to anybody of my own kind and age? London never had any formal or obvious beauty, such as you find in Paris; or any great, overwhelming grandeur, such as Rome has. But the districts for which I loved her, and several other districts too, had a queer beauty of their own, and were intensely characteristic—inalienably Londonish. To an intelligent foreigner, visiting London for the first time, what would you hasten to show? Except some remnants here and there, and some devious little nooks, there is nothing that would excite or impress him. The general effect of the buildings that have sprung up everywhere in recent years is not such an effect as the intelligent foreigner may not have seen in divers other places—Chicago, for example, or Berlin, or Pittsburgh. London has been cosmopolitanised, democratised, commercialised, mechanised, standardised, vulgarised, so extensively that one's pride in showing it to a foreigner is changed to a wholesome humility. One feels rather as Virgil may have felt in showing Hell to Dante.

It is a bright, cheerful, salubrious Hell, certainly. But still—to *my* mind—Hell. In some ways a better place, I readily concede, than it was in my day, and in days before mine. Heinrich Heine was horrified by the poverty—the squalor and starvation—that abounded in the midst of the immense wealth and splendour. Some years later Gavarni's soul was shocked by it; and then Dostoievsky's; and presently Monsieur Ludovic Halévy's; and in due course Mr. Henry James's. I too am human. I am therefore glad that Seven Dials—and similar places which I used to skirt with romantic horror—are gone. Had I been acting as guide to those distinguished visitors, I should have tried to convince them that no such places existed, save in the creative alien fancy. But I ask myself: Suppose those illustrious visitors rose from their graves to-day and asked me to show them round the sights that would best please their æsthetic sensibilities in the London of this year of grace, what should I say, what do, in my patriotic embarrassment? I suppose I would, with vague waves of the hand, stammeringly redirect them to their graves.

I could not ask them to accompany me along Piccadilly or up Park Lane, to admire the vast excesses of contemporary architecture. I could not say to them, 'Never mind the rasure of certain unassuming houses that were called "great houses" in your day—and in mine. Cast up your eyes—up, up, up!—at the houses that have displaced them. Try to count the little uniform slits that serve as windows in the splendid ferro-concrete surface. Admire the austerity of the infinite *ensemble*. Think how inspiring to the historic imagination it will all be, a century or so hence!' I couldn't speak thus, for I cannot imagine any history being made in these appallingly bleak yet garish tenements. Or, at any rate, I refuse to suppose that they or any of the similar monstrosities that have been springing up in all the more eligible districts could ever take on an historic tone. They will continue to look like—what shall I say? —what *do* they look like?—improper workhouses.

Odious though they are in themselves, one might not hate them much if one found them on some barren plain in (say) the middle-west of America—some plain as barren and as meaningless as they. But when one thinks of the significant houses, the old habitable homes, that were demolished to make way for them, and when one sees how what remains of decent human architecture is reduced by them to the scale of hardly noticeable hovels, then one's heart sickens, and one's tongue curses the age into which one has survived. A few years ago, in the Print Room of the British Museum, Mr. Laurence Binyon showed me a very ancient little water-colour drawing. The foreground of it was a rather steep grassy slope. At the foot of the slope stood a single building, which I at once recognised as St. James's Palace. Beyond the Palace were stretches of green meadows; and far away there was just one building—the Abbey of Westminster. And I thought how pained the artist would have been if he had foreseen the coming of St. James's Street. I felt sure that he, like myself, preferred the country to any town. Yet I could not find it in my heart to deplore the making of that steep little street, destined to be so full of character and history. I could only regret that my favourite street was being steadily degraded, year after year, by the constructive vandals. There are no actual skyscrapers in it, as yet. But already the Palace cuts a poor figure. And the lovely façade of Boodle's is sadly squat. And a certain little old but ever young shop that stands somewhere between those two is hardly visible to the naked eye. I would affectionately name it, were I not so anxious to obey the B.B.C.'s admirable ban on that greatest of all modern pests, the advertiser.

Regent Street, Nash's masterpiece, which is mourned so bitterly by so many people, was never very dear to my heart, even before the days when Norman Shaw's pseudo-Florentine fortress suddenly sprang up and ruined the scale of its quadrant and of all the rest of it. Its tone was always rather vulgar. It was never anything but a happy hunting-ground for ardent shoppers. Nothing but shopping had ever happened in it. But it was a noble design. And when its wide road and pavements were empty in the dawn, and its level copings were pale against the smokeless sky, the great long strong curve of the smooth-faced houses had a beauty that I shall not forget. I conceive that the pretentious chaos now reigning in its stead must in the quiet magic of the dawn be especially nasty.

It was the Squares, that particular glory of London, that I loved best of all. Their green centres have not yet been built over, for some reason. I look with pleasure at their surviving grass and trees. But I try not to see from the corners of my eyes what has happened to their architecture. St. James's Square, the finest of them all, has been wrecked utterly. Berkeley Square, which was a good second, has suffered a like fate. So has Portman Square. Dear little Kensington Square has been saved, by the obstinacy of some enlightened tenants, from the clutches of Mammon. Bedford Square is intact, as yet. Let us be thankful, before it is too late, for much of Bloomsbury. The London University is about to play the deuce there. I suppose the Inns of Court, those four sanctuaries of civilisation, are safe in the adroit hands of the lawyers. Parliament will not be able to betray *them,* as she has betrayed that other sanctuary, the Adelphi.

I revisit England and London at intervals of two or three years; and every time I find that the havoc that has been wrought in my absence is more than ever extensive. How do I contrive to bear it? Let me reveal that secret. As I go my rounds, I imagine that the present is the past. I imagine myself a man of the twenty-first century, a person with an historic sense, whose prayer that he should behold the London of a hundred years ago has been granted. And my heart is thrilled with rapture. Look! There's a horse drawing a cart! And look! There's a quite small house—a lovely little thing that looks as though it had been built by the hand of man, and as though a man might quite pleasantly live in it. It has a chimney, with smoke coming out of it. And there's a coal-heaver. And there's—it must be—it *is*—a muffin-man!

By such devices of make-believe do I somewhat console and brace myself. But there is always a dead-weight of sadness in me. Selfish sadness: I ought to keep my pity for the young people who never saw what I have seen, who will live to see what I shall not see—future great vistas of more and more commercialism, more machinery, more standardisation, more nullity.

I warned you that I was going to be depressing. I wish I hadn't kept my word. I might well have broken it on an evening so soon after Christmas, so soon before the New Year. Forget this talk. Or at any rate discount it. Remember that after all I'm an old fogey—and perhaps rather an old fool. And let me assure you that I'm cheerful company enough whenever I'm not in London and not thinking of London. And now I'm just off to the country. I have arranged to be driven straight from Broadcasting House to Paddington. I shall *just* catch the train.—I wish you all a very happy New Year—somewhere in the country.—I hope I haven't advertised Paddington.—Ladies and Gentlemen, goodnight.

SPEED

(1936)

SPEED

(Sunday evening, April 26th, 1936.)

In the Eye of the Lord,
By the Will of the Lord,
Out of the infinite
Bounty dissembled,
Since Time began,
In the Hand of the Lord,
Speed!

Speed as a chattel:
Speed in your daily
Account and economy;
One with your wines,
And your books and your bath—
Speed!
Speed as a rapture:
An integral element
In the new scheme of Life
Which the good Lord, the Master,
Wills well you should frame
In the light of His laugh
And His great, His ungrudging
His reasoned benevolence—
Speed!

These words, ladies and gentlemen, are not mine. They are the words of a man far more remarkable than I: William Ernest Henley, poet and critic, editor of 'The Scots Observer', a great inspirer of youth. The light of his fame is dim now; but it shone fiercely in the eighteen-nineties, and after. He himself was a fierce fellow enough. He had the head of a Viking, and the torso of a Viking; but from his early manhood he had been crippled by ill-health, insomuch that he could walk only with the help of crutches—he, who should have gone ever swinging over hill and dale, to satiate his vitality. In the very early years of this century, in the very early days of motoring, young Mr. Alfred Harmsworth, who was one of his great admirers, took him out for a long drive into the country. At last Henley went swinging over hill and dale. The Mercédès was for him a glorious revelation, an apocalypse. His Muse vibrantly responded, and he wrote the fine poem of which I have read to you the opening lines.

In those days even a quite prosaic and quite agile person, seated in a motor-car, felt something of that fine frenzy which filled Henley's breast. Cars were not the things they are now. You didn't have to creep into them and crouch *in* them and squirm *out of* them. They were wide-open to the elements, and wind-screens were unknown. And in fine dry weather, as you sped along the roads at what seemed then a terrific pace, the air rushed into your lungs with the utmost violence, making a new man of you—and a better man of you. So as not to be blinded with dust, you wore large goggles over your eyes. But dust entered into your ears and nostrils and into the very pores of your skin. And all the while you were moving not forward merely. The machine was such that you were continuously bobbing up and down, and oscillating from side to side. Your body was taking an immense amount of wholesome exercise. Insomuch that when the ride was over, and you had gone and vigorously shampooed the dust away from you, you felt that you were now an even newer and a still better man.

I, at any rate, used to have that conviction about myself. And if I had been a poet—and a generaliser, as every poet is—I should doubtless have tried to found on my experience some great philosophic moral. Henley was not content to have had a joy-ride. The joy of his ride had to be brought into close relation to the cosmos. It must be shown that the life of mankind on this planet had been immensely and for ever enriched by the internal combustion engine. Said Henley:

> The heart of Man
> Tears at Man's destiny
> Ever; and ever
> Makes what it may
> Of his wretched occasions,
> His infinitesimal
> Portion in Time.
>
> Hence the Mercédès!

And by the discovery of the Mercédès our portion in Time was to be very appreciably and very agreeably magnified.

Henley had not any religion of an ecclesiastical kind. But he was nevertheless a deeply religious man. He had made a god of Literature. He had made a god of the British Empire. He had made a god also of the Tory Party. And here was a new god for him—Speed. If someone had asked him whether the invention of the steam-engine and the railroad had greatly blessed our lot, he might have looked rather dubious. For he was, despite his Imperialism, essentially an eighteenth-century man, and Victorian things did not arride him. But his faith in the universal beneficence of the Mercédès showed that he was, after all, in one respect, rather belatedly, a true Victorian. He believed, as we, alas!—we distressful moderns—no longer do, in the idea of Progress. I rather doubt whether, if he were living today, in a world that has succumbed so meekly to the ideal of speed—speed everywhere and at all times, produced by means of machinery and regarded as an end in itself—he would maintain that we had added a cubit to our stature.

In a sense, mankind has always loved speed. Speed here and there, speed in season, has always been acknowledged to be great fun. The Marathon race was a very popular institution. So were the Roman chariot races. One is probably right in supposing that Adam and Eve used often to race each other round the Garden of Eden, very blithely. Dick Turpin's exploit on Black Bess would have commended itself in any era to the people of any nation. So would even the involuntary adventure of John Gilpin. Dear to us all is the thought of Puck putting a girdle round the earth in forty minutes. Long live the Derby, and the Grand National! All honour to young Mr. Timpson, of Trinity College, Cambridge, who walked, the other day, to St. Paul's Cathedral and back in twenty-three hours, for a wager. Even that occasional squadron of stockbrokers marching from London to an hotel in Brighton rather thrills the heart . . . or doesn't it? Charles Dickens never wrote anything more exhilarating than the Pickwickians' journey by coach to Rochester. De Quincey was at his very best on the subject of the Eclipse coach. Coaches seem, indeed, to have been a godsend to all novelists and essayists. There was magic in them, evidently. They are not romantic to us alone: they were so to their contemporaries. Railway-trains were romantic for a few years. In the memoirs or diaries of the Victorians you will find that the first journey by rail made as deep a dint on sensibility as did the Duke of Wellington's funeral, or the first visit to the Crystal Palace. Well might those early passengers have prayed,

> Lord, send a man like Bobbie Burns
> To sing the Song of Steam!

But many years were to elapse before Mr. Kipling came, combining with an immense gift for verse a mystical adoration of machinery. 'Romance brought up the nine-fifteen,' said Mr. Kipling. But, we ask ourselves, did it? Wasn't it rather the engine-man and the stoker? And we ask ourselves whether they perhaps are romantic figures, and we hope that we can answer in the affirmative; but—well, it would seem that in machinery there is for most of us something non-conductive of emotion. A man on a horse, galloping hell-for-leather, or a man driving a pair or more of horses in like manner, a man running like an arrow from the bow, a man sailing a boat in a great gale, strikes a chord in us and is a promising subject for literary art. So would be a man flying fast through the empyrean by means of a pair of natural wings. But the man in the aeroplane or in the motor-boat or in the motor-car is somehow less inspiring—recent and fresh though he is, and eagerly waiting to have masterpieces written about him by poets and essayists and novelists. May those masterpieces be written soon! I shall welcome them the more heartily for not having expected them.

Mental speed is a thing which, like speed of limb, has always commanded admiration. We are glad that Lope de Vega wrote fifteen hundred plays. We wish our Shakespeare had done likewise, but console ourselves by the report that 'he never blotted a line.' It gratifies us that Father Newman wrote his lovely *Apologia* in eight weeks, and Samuel Johnson his fine *Rasselas* in the evenings of one week. We should be inspirited by any evidence that Edward Gibbon wrote the *Decline and Fall of the Roman Empire* in six months, or that Christopher Wren designed St. Paul's Cathedral in twenty-five minutes. And oh, how we should rejoice to find that the rapidity of transport that is now at our disposal had duly accelerated the pace at which our brains work! We are ashamed that our thoughts form themselves no more swiftly than in the old restful days. I have an impression that most people do talk rather faster than when I was young. They certainly eat much faster; insomuch that if I am invited to meet some of them at luncheon or dinner I find at each course that I have only just begun when they have all finished; and when I reach my home I ask, 'Are there any biscuits?' Perhaps this general quickness of mastication is a sign of greater athleticism. But it may be due merely to the fact that people have so much to do now. One hears much of unemployment. But most of the people whom I meet now are employed somewhere, and after luncheon must hurry back to the places they came from. That is a very wholesome state of things. But, as a good listener, I rather sigh for the old leisurely repasts and the habit of lingering long after them to hear more from the lips of such talkers as Oscar Wilde or Henry James, Reginald Turner or Charles Brookfield—and then strolling home, well-satisfied, along the uncrowded pavements and across the quite safe roads.

Quite safe roads. Rather an arresting phrase, that! I can imagine that in more than one home some listening-in child has just exclaimed, 'Oh, mother, were roads ever safe?' And perhaps the mother is at this moment telling the child that they once were—instead of listening to *me*. Perhaps she would rather *not* listen to me. Roads are a painful subject nowadays. They are railroads without rails. They are so not only in London, but all over the British Isles. They are so in every country and every city all over the world. They are places for motorists only. And the motorists themselves are not comfortable on them.

The other day, a motoristic friend of mine was complaining to me bitterly, even violently, about the behaviour of pedestrians. They were abominably careless and stupid, he insisted. I hate to see anyone agitated by a grievance, and I tried to soothe my friend by an appeal to reason. I said, 'No doubt we pedestrians are very trying. But you must remember that, after all, we were on the roads for many, many centuries before you came along in your splendid car. And remember, it isn't we that are threatening to kill *you*. It is you that are threatening to kill *us*. And if we are rather flustered, and occasionally do the wrong thing, you should make allowances—and, if the worst comes to the worst, lay some flowers on our graves.'

We are constantly told by the Press that we must be 'traffic-conscious'. But there is really no need to tell us we must be so. How could we be otherwise? How not be concussion-apprehensive, annihilation-evasive, and similar compound words? When the children of this generation, brought up in fear, shall have become adult, what sort of nervous ailments will their progeny have, one wonders? Many of the present children won't grow up at all. Very old people and very young people form the majority of those who are annually slaughtered upon our roads.

Statistics do not travel well through the air; so I shall spare you them. Nor is the air a very good vehicle for moral indignation. Tub-thumping is apt to fail there. The listener cannot see the tub, nor the fist, nor the flashing eye. But I do hope that orators on platforms are magnetically orating, all the time, about the habitual carnage; and I hope that the clergy of all denominations express themselves likewise in their pulpits, every Sunday. For I think you need rousing. You are ashamed that in years not very remote from ours young women were worked to death in the factories, and children in the coal-mines. You blush at the barbarities of criminal justice in the eighteenth and early nineteenth centuries. What do you think posterity will think of *this* age?

'Perhaps,' you say, 'posterity will be worse than we are.' Well, then, let us set a good example to posterity. Let us persuade our legislators that we are shocked by the present state of things. Let us suggest to them that they may lose votes if they are not as shocked as we are. Let us insinuate that tests far more exacting than the present tests should be imposed on anyone who desires a licence to drive a motor-car. Let us whisper that the system by which a motorist can insure himself against any loss by his own carelessness is not a very good system. Let us, slightly raising our voices, demand that a driver convicted of dangerous driving should be liable to a much longer term of imprisonment than he is now. Let us—but all this is merely tinkering with the problem. The main root of the mischief is that great fetish of ours, Speed.

I have friends who argue brilliantly, and in perfect sincerity, that Speed in itself is no danger. They say that if the traffic were slower than it is the number of accidents would be increased. And they quote figures, and draw diagrams, and are as able as they are technical; and I am very much bewildered. If a man said to me, 'Oh, well, England is very much over-populated,' or 'The Orientals don't attach the same value to life as we do; and they are notoriously wiser than we are—though they've always been so slow in comparison with us,' I should understand his point of view, though I should not share it. Nor do I dispute the proposition that Speed in itself is no danger. A cannon-ball fired from a cannon is not in itself dangerous. It is dangerous only if you happen to be in the way of it. You would like to step out of its way; but there is no time for you to do so. Perhaps it would like to stop short of you; but it can't: it is going too fast. That is what motorists are doing even when in 'built-up areas' they obey the speed-limit of thirty miles an hour. They are going too fast. It would be unreasonable to expect them to impose on themselves a speed-limit of twenty miles an hour. But this is the limit which should—and sooner or later will be—imposed on them. Whether this slowing-down of traffic will cause a great or a small loss of national income, is, I am told, a point on which expert economists are not agreed. What is certain is that it will save annually a vast number of lives.

At first, of course, there will be much wailing and gnashing of teeth. The motorists will be frightfully sorry for themselves. And those of you who are not motorists will feel rather sorry for *them.* Rather sorry for yourselves too, perhaps. You will feel that there has been a great act of desecration: hands have been laid on the Ark of the Covenant: the divinity of Jazz has been impugned.

But here is a heartening fact for you. We are all of us travelling at a tremendous rate, and we shall always continue to do so. We shall not, it is true, be able to get rid of our speed-limit. But it is a very liberal one. 1,110 miles a minute is not a limit to be grumbled at. Our planet is not truly progressing, of course: it is back at its starting-point every year. But it never for an instant pauses in its passage through space. Nor will it do so even when, some billions of years hence, it shall have become too cold for us human beings to exist upon its surface. It will still be proceeding at its present pace: *1,110 miles a minute.*

This, ladies and gentlemen, is indeed a beautiful and a consoling thought—a thought for you to sleep on, to dream of. Sleep well. Dream beautifully. In fact—Good Night.

A SMALL BOY SEEING GIANTS

(1936)

A SMALL BOY SEEING GIANTS

(*Sunday evening, July 26th, 1936.*)

Ladies and Gentlemen,—The title that has just been announced to you is perhaps rather cryptic. And as I am not a young poet, and have not that lovely modesty which forbids the young poet to think that his meaning could matter twopence to anybody on this earth, I hasten to explain that the Small Boy is myself—or rather *was* myself, half a century ago; and that the Giants were some more or less elderly Liberal or Conservative gentlemen who governed England in those days. They were my great hobby. I might almost say that they were my passion. I hadn't the honour of knowing any of them personally. But I knew them all by sight. And it was always with rapture that I saw them.

In my earlier years, soldiers had monopolised the romantic side of me. Although, like all my coævals, I wore a sailor suit, my heart was with the land forces; insomuch that I insisted on wearing also, out of doors, a belt with a sword attached to it, and on my breast a medal which, though it had merely the Crystal Palace embossed on it, I associated with the march to Kandahar. I used to watch with emotion the sentries changing guard outside Kensington Palace; and it was my purpose to be one of them hereafter. Meanwhile I made many feeble little drawings of them, which I coloured strongly. But somehow, mysteriously, when I was eight years old or so, the soldiery was eclipsed for me by the constabulary. Somehow the scarlet and the bearskins began to thrill me less than the austere costume and calling of the Metropolitan Police. Once in every two hours a policeman came, on his beat, past the house of my parents. At the window of the dining-room I would await his coming, punctually behold him with profound interest, and watch him out of sight. It was not the daffodils that marked for me the coming of the season of Spring. It was the fact that policemen suddenly wore short tunics with steel buttons. It was not the fall of the leaf nor the swallows' flight that signalled Autumn to me. It was the fact that policemen were wearing long thick frock-coats with buttons of copper. But even more than in the day-time did policemen arrest me, as it were, in the watches of the night. The dark lantern was the truly great, the irresistible thing about them. More than once, from the window of my night-nursery, I had seen that lantern flashed at opposite front doors and through area-railings. My paintings of policemen were mostly nocturnes—a dim, helmeted figure with a long white ray of light. Although I possessed, of course, a dark lantern of my own, and used it much, I preferred my occasional glimpses of the genuine article, and looked forward impatiently to being a member of the Force. But the young are faithless. By the time I was eleven years old I despised the Force. I was interested only in politicians—in Statesmen, as they were called at that time.

I had already, for some years, been aware of them. I had seen them, two-dimensionally and on a small scale, every Wednesday, in the pages of *Punch*, and had in a remote and tepid way revered them. I had not thought of them as actual, live men. Rather, they were, as portrayed in the cartoons of the great John Tenniel, nobly mythical to me. Sometimes they wore togas; but more often they wore chitons and breastplates, and were wielding or brandishing swords. Their shins were protected by greaves, and their calves were immensely muscular; and in the matter of biceps they were unsurpassable. They were Ajaxes and Hectors and Achilleses. Now and then they rose to greater heights, becoming Herculeses, Vulcans, Marses and the like. *Punch* was firmly Gladstonian in its politics; and therefore the Prime Minister was always more muscular than any of his enemies, redoubtable though they too were; and the attitudes that he struck were more striking than theirs. I didn't quite like this. For my father was a Conservative, and so, accordingly, was I. I wished—though I didn't care enough to pray—for the downfall of Gladstone. Some time in the year 1883 I read a speech delivered in the House of Commons by Lord Randolph Churchill. I felt that here was the man to compass the downfall; for he was so very rude. Even the best-behaved little boys rejoice in the rudeness of other people. Lord Randolph's rudeness in a good cause refreshed my young heart greatly; nor ever did his future speeches disappoint me. But, much though I delighted in him, I didn't quite think of him as an actual person. I thought of him as Phaëton. Tenniel—or was it Linley Sambourne?—had depicted him as Phaëton, standing ready on the ground while old Sir Stafford Northcote (the leader of the Opposition, here depicted as Phoebus

Apollo) was driving the chariot of the sun. I resented the cartoonist's analogy. But the physical image abode with me.

It was the London Stereoscopic Company that first opened my eyes to the fact that Churchill and Gladstone, Northcote and Harcourt, Chamberlain, Hartington and all those others were actual, mortal, modern men. Not until I was nearly twelve did I inspect that great long double window on the eastern side of Regent Street, famous for its galaxy of photographs of eminent personages. The place of honour was accorded of course to members of the Royal Family. But precedence over Archbishops and Bishops, Generals, Admirals, Poets, Actors and Actresses, was taken by the Statesmen, as we no longer call them. Not even to Lord Tennyson and Sir Garnet Wolseley and Mr. Henry Irving and Miss Connie Gilchrist was accorded such prominence as to the least of these. For these were giants in those days. They were not perhaps Gods, but they certainly were Titans, in the public eye. And here they all were in *my* eye, tailored and hosier'd as men. With luck, I might some day see one of them in the street. I studied the portraits keenly. I fixed the features in my mind. I stayed there long. And on my way home I saw a man who was unmistakably—Mr. Childers. To you, Ladies and Gentlemen, I suppose his name means nothing. But he was at that time Chancellor of the Exchequer. It was a great, a throbbing moment.

Of Mr. Childers I made several drawings—very unpromising little drawings—when I reached my home. And thereafter, in the course of my holidays from school, I drew many of his colleagues. When a Cabinet Council was to be held, the fact was usually announced by the morning papers of that day. And there at the hour appointed, there on the pavement of Downing Street, opposite to No. 10, would be I, awaiting breathlessly the advent of the Giants. The greatest and most awful of them all would of course be invisible. Mr. Gladstone was somewhere behind those brown brick walls. But the others would be vouchsafed to me, one of them coming perhaps from the direction of Parliament Street, another from the courtyard of the Government Offices behind me, another up the flight of steps from St. James's Park. They are dead, one and all of them. Most of them died very many years ago. While I stood staring at them, Mr. Asquith was unknown to them : he was just a barrister in fairly good practice. The present Father of the House of Commons, Mr. Lloyd George, was a young solicitor, roaming nightly with bare feet and dreamful eyes along the clouded ridges of the Welsh mountains and hailing the roseate dawn. Mr. Baldwin was at Harrow. A quite recent President of the Oxford Union, Mr. George Nathaniel Curzon, was travelling observantly in the waste spaces of Siam and of Korea. Mr. Edward Carson was just beginning to make a name for himself in the Irish police-courts. Mr. Austen Chamberlain was at Trinity College, Cambridge. Mr. Neville Chamberlain was at Rugby. Mr. Winston Churchill was a pugnacious and not very happy little boy at a preparatory school. Many, many years were to elapse before Mr. Duff Cooper and Mr. Anthony Eden, Mr. Harold Nicolson and Mr. A. P. Herbert, were summoned forth from among the infinite ranks of the unborn. I am what the writers of obituary notices call 'an interesting link with the past'.

I wish I could have foreseen the future. Had I done so—had I known how exactly, how furtively like one another our rulers would try to look—I should have revelled even more than I did revel at the sight of those men of 1884. Visually, they let themselves go, without self-consciousness or fear. Each one of them was a law unto himself. Some of them—Lord Kimberley, for example, and Mr. Dodson—had beards without moustaches. Some of them were clean-shaven. One of them, Mr. Shaw-Lefevre, had always what looked like a four days' growth of beard. Lord Hartington's beard and moustache were far longer than Sir Charles Dilke's. Mr. Joseph Chamberlain was content with small side-whiskers. Sir William Harcourt had a 'Newgate frill'. So had Lord Northbrook, who wore, however and moreover, a becoming tuft on the chin. The wide, pale, pleasantly roguish face of old Lord Granville was framed in masses of silvery curls. Some wore their hair long, others short. Some of them dressed badly, others—in an off-hand way—well. To none of them except Chamberlain and Dilke, those two harbingers of another age, would one have applied the epithet *neat*. Believe me, they offered no end of latitude to the limner.

Spiritually, nevertheless, they bore strong likenesses to one another. Barring the two harbingers, and barring of course Mr. Gladstone, who was a creature apart, not to be fitted into any category whatsoever, they were authentic Whigs, one and all; eighteenth-century men, despite their date. Some of them were old enough to have dined, often, at Holland House. Not one of them, I feel sure, had failed to breakfast frequently with Mr. Samuel Rogers. The new Government Offices were still new to them, and

I expect they admired those buildings greatly. They remembered the time when Downing Street had lodging-houses in it, and a tavern or two, and a milliner's shop—things inconsonant with the affairs of a great nation. I daresay they regretted that Nos. 10 and 11 had not been demolished and rebuilt in the grandiose modern fashion. What charm would the Eighteenth Century have had for gentlemen who were a part of it? The love of by-gone things is a quite recent growth —due mainly to the fact that we have fallen on evil times. If we could all of us follow Mr. H. G. Wells's good example, dismiss the present from our minds, and fix our eyes steadfastly on the future, then we could share his wholesome contempt for the past. But we can't. We are morbid. I, perhaps, more so than most of us. Some weeks ago, as I was passing through St. James's Park, I looked up towards the street that I had so fondly haunted in my childhood—the street of the Giants. I ascended the steps to it and stood again before No. 10, gazing. 'This sweet corner' Horace Walpole had called it in a letter written by him therefrom to Sir Horace Mann. 'Sweet' is a trivial epithet, but one must remember that Horace's father, Sir Robert, had no preceding Giant in that corner: only a little of history had been made there as yet; the rest was to come. I gazed at the house of Pitt and Palmerston, Disraeli, Gladstone, and all those others; at the narrow front-door, with the unassuming fanlight above it; at the lantern in the traceries of the wrought-iron 'overthrow' beneath which so many Giants had stepped so long before I was born. And then my eye was attracted by a grey-blue placard in one of the two hall-windows. I crossed the road to read it . . .

Garden Party
Mrs. Stanley Baldwin
At Home
at No. 10, Downing Street
in aid of
The Safer Motherhood Appeal
Tuesday July 14
when the world's greatest
male ensemble of 35 performers
The Don Cossack Choir
with their famous conductor
Sarge Jaroff
will make their one appearance in London this season
Tickets £2. 2. 0

These words I read with surprise, but with entire sympathy. Here was an excellent cause to support, a very good use for the old garden to be put to. Had I been rich enough, I would have bought a ticket. But I rather wondered what Horace Walpole would have had to say in the matter. Something supercilious, something flippant, I am afraid. He was rather inhuman.

I wished I could see again those old Gladstonian figures—and the Salisburyans who succeeded to them in '85: the distinguished and formidable figure of Sir Michael Hicks-Beach; the distinguished and venerable figure of Lord John Manners, that last survivor of the Young England movement, whom Miss Charlotte Brontë, when as a young man he visited Haworth parsonage, had thought so handsome; above all, the distinguished and attractive figure of Lord Randolph, my chosen hero. He seemed, in some ways, always rather out of the picture. He seemed young for

Downing Street, and had the air of a man of fashion rather than of affairs. He alone wore a moustache without beard or whiskers—an arrangement suggestive of levity. His was the only top-hat that was ironed, and it was ironed to the utmost lustre. He alone smoked cigarettes, and he smoked them through a very long amber mouthpiece. He, and only he, sometimes wore a buttonhole. Sometimes he looked as happy and insouciant as Mr. Gladstone's young disciple, Lord Rosebery; at other times, and oftener, he looked as tragically sad as did Lord Rosebery in later years. Very different though the two men were in character, they had points in common. The gods had bestowed on both of them shining gifts of mind and of speech, and had foredoomed them both to fail irretrievably.

There is much to be said for failure. It is more interesting than success. Rosebery and Randolph Churchill are, among the office-holders of their generation, the only two that still hold our attention and stir our curiosity. Lord Salisbury, their elder contemporary, is a noble, a monumental figure which does not detain us. It may be that if the veteran Mr. Gladstone had carried Home Rule he would be rather less detentive than he now is. For some time after his death we tended to depreciate him. Three or four years ago I was amused by a conversation between two political ladies of fashion, one an Asquithian Liberal, the other a Tory. The Liberal one, after having spoken of Mr. Gladstone with enthusiasm, said, 'But of course people only talk of Dizzy now. Gladstone's forgotten.' The Tory one said, 'Oh—I thought he was rather comin' in again, dear?' She was right. Mr. Gladstone is once more with us. Here he is, the mystical realist. Dizzy, the sceptical idealist, is rather further away. Dizzy is, of course—Dizzy always was—irresistible. His novels, his phrases, some of his speeches even, can still delight us deeply. His imagination and his wit are glorious, as was his patience. But he lacks something. In the last year of his life, speaking to one of the members of the Fourth Party, he said, 'I fully appreciate your feelings, but you must stick to Northcote. He represents the respectability of the Party. I wholly sympathise with you all, because *I* was never respectable.' Nor has he become so. We can revel in him; but we cannot respect him. There is something unreal, something absurd about him. In this unrestful and threatened age of the world's history we are moved to hanker after the moral force and fervour, and the endless vitality of Gladstone. We want a Gladstone *de nos jours.*

I saw him only three times. Once from the Strangers' Gallery in the House of Commons, early in 1885; and then and there, for the first and last time, I also heard him. He was merely answering a question about procedure, but he spoke for not less than a couple of minutes, in low tones, leaning far forward, with hands outspread upon the table, and ever turning from side to side and around, envisaging the whole assembly. Though I regarded him as a great power for evil, he fascinated, he won me. The second time was a year or so later. I was one of the crowd that assembled in Parliament Square when he was about to introduce the first Home Rule Bill. There were boos among the cheers as he drove past, beside his wife, in an open landau, gravely bowing, his great dark eyes very wide open in his ivory-white old face. I was not among the booers. I cheered—in spite of myself—wildly. The third time, I was an undergraduate, standing on the steps outside the Sheldonian Theatre, in which building Mr. Gladstone, after long absence from Oxford, was to lecture on the Homeric poems. The Vice-Chancellor's brougham punctually arrived, and out of it stepped the Vice-Chancellor and, in his D.C.L. robes, Mr. Gladstone, bareheaded, amidst a tumultuous welcome. He ascended the steps, dark-eyed, white-faced, smiling; very old, but stalwart; he turned, stood, bowed slowly, deeply, from side to side, to the crowd below. He had bowed to many crowds, in his day, but never to one that loved him more than this one. I associate him always with Oxford.

And it was with Oxford—more, even, than with Scotland, I think—that he especially associated himself. When he lay dying, the Hebdomadal Council sent to him a message of regard and affection. 'To this,' says his biographer, John Morley, 'he listened most attentively and over it brooded long, then he dictated to his youngest daughter sentence by sentence his reply: "There is no expression of Christian sympathy that I could value more than that of the ancient University of Oxford, the God-fearing and God-sustaining University of Oxford. I served her, perhaps mistakenly, but to the best of my ability. My most earnest prayers are with her to the uttermost and to the last."'

These are grand words. With them let me close my discourse. I said at the outset that I was an interesting link with the past. Perhaps that was begging the question. I claim merely that I am a link with the past. If I have bored you, forgive me. And be of good cheer. This is the last time that I shall have the honour of addressing you, for the present. I am going to Italy, to my home, and shall not soon be here again. And so I wish you not only Goodnight, but also Goodbye.

MUSIC HALLS OF MY YOUTH

(1942)

MUSIC HALLS OF MY YOUTH

(*Sunday evening at ten o'clock, 18th January, 1942.*)

Ladies and Gentlemen, or—if you prefer that mode of address—G'deevning.

It is past my bed-time; for when one is very old one reverts to the habits of childhood, and goes to bed quite early—though not quite so early as one went to one's night-nursery; and not by command, but just of one's own accord, without any kicking or screaming. I always hear the nine o'clock news and the postscript; but soon after these I am in bed and asleep. I take it that my few elders and most of my contemporaries will have switched off and retired ere now, and that you who are listening to me are either in the prime of life or in the flush of enviable youth, and will therefore know little of the subject on which I am going to dilate with senile garrulity.

Would that those others had sat up to hear me! In them I could have struck the fond, the vibrant chords of memory. To instruct is a dreary function. I should have liked to thrill, to draw moisture to the eyes. But, after all, you do, all of you, know *something* of my theme. The historic sense bloweth where it listeth, and in the past few years there has been a scholarly revival of interest in the kind of melodies which I had supposed were to lie in eternal oblivion. Some forty years ago that enlightened musician, Cecil Sharp, was ranging around remote parts of England

and coaxing eldest inhabitants in ingle-nooks to quaver out folk-songs that only they remembered. It was a great good work that Cecil Sharp did in retrieving for us so many beautiful old tunes and poems—poems and tunes in which are enshrined for us a happier and better life than ours, a life lived under the auspices of Nature. I salute his memory. And I take leave to think that he would have been as glad—well, almost as glad—as I am to hear often, on the wireless, revocations of things warbled across the footlights of Music Halls in decades long ago. For these too are folk-songs, inalienably English, and racy of—no, not of the soil, but of the pavements from which they sprang. I even take leave to think that if Shakespeare had lived again and had heard them warbled in the Halls he might have introduced them into his plays, just as he had introduced—with magical variations, of course—the folk-songs of his own time. He might have done so. Or again, he might *not*. For he was very keen, poor man, on a thing which many of the younger poets of our day disapprove of, as being in rather bad taste: the element of beauty. And I cannot claim that this element was to be found in the songs of the 'Lion Comique' or of the 'Serio' of my day, or of the days before mine. Indeed, I cannot claim for these ditties much more than that there was in them a great gusto. But gusto is an immense virtue. Gusto goes a huge long way.

'My day', as I have called it, dawned exactly fifty-one years ago. I was a callow undergraduate, in my first Christmas vacation. I had been invited to dine at the Café Royal by my brother Julius, whose age was twice as great as mine; and after dinner he proposed that we should go to the Pavilion Music

Hall, where a man called Chevalier had just made his début, and had had a great success. I was filled with an awful, but pleasant, sense of audacity in venturing into such a place, so plebeian and unhallowed a den, as a Music Hall; and I was relieved, though slightly disappointed also, at finding that the Pavilion seemed very like a theatre, except that the men around us were mostly smoking, and not in evening clothes, and that there was alongside of the stalls an extensive drinking-bar, of which the barmaids were the only—or almost the only—ladies present, and that the stage was occupied by one man only. One and only, but great: none other than The Great MacDermott, of whom I had often heard in my childhood as the singer of '*We Don't Want To Fight, But, By Jingo, If We Do*'. And here he was, in the flesh, in the grease-paint, surviving and thriving, to my delight; a huge old burly fellow, with a yellow wig and a vast expanse of crumpled shirt-front that had in the middle of it a very large, not *very* real diamond stud. And he was still belligerent, wagging a great imperative forefinger at us across the footlights, and roaring in a voice slightly husky but still immensely powerful a song with the refrain 'That's What We'd Like To Do!' In Russia there had been repressive measures against Nihilists, and Mr. Joseph Hatton had written a book entitled 'By Order of the Czar'—a book that created a great sensation. And in consequence of it the Great MacDermott had been closeted with the Prime Minister; nor did he treat the interview as confidential. I remember well some words of his song.

'"What would you like to do, my Lord?"
I asked Lord Salisburee'——

but the words need the music; and I remember the music quite well too. A pity I can't sing it. But perhaps I could do a croaking suggestion of it . . .

(*Sung*) '"What would you like to do, my Lord?"
  I asked Lord Salisburee.
"The great Election's very near,
  And where will then you be?
The English people have the right
  To fight for those who are
Being oppressed and trodden down
  By Order of the Czar.
That's what we'd like to do!
  Beware lest we do it too!
To join those aspirants
  Who'd crush Russian tyrants——
That's what we'd like to do!"'

And I do assure you that the audience would have liked to do it. You may wonder at that, after hearing my voice. You would not have wondered had you heard the Great MacDermott's.

But the fierce mood was short-lived. There arose in the firmament another luminary. Albert Chevalier, as new as MacDermott was old, came shining forth amidst salvoes of fervid expectation. A very elastic and electric little creature, with twists and turns of face and body and voice as many as the innumerable pearl buttons that adorned his jacket and his breeches. Frankly fantastic, but nevertheless very real, very human and loveable in his courtship of 'Arriet by moonlight, or in his enjoyment of the neighbours' good wishes as he drove his little donkey-chaise along the Old Kent Road. I was at that time too young to appreciate the subtleties of the technique that he had acquired and matured on the legitimate stage. But in later years I knew enough to realise that he was becoming rather a slave to these subtleties. He was no longer content to merge his acting in the singing of a song. He acted outside the song, acted at leisure between the notes, letting lilt and rhythm go to the deuce. But his composition of words and music never became less good. There was always a firm basic idea, a clear aspect of human character. 'My Old Dutch', 'The Little Nipper', 'You can't Get a Roise out o' Oi', and the rest of them, still live for that reason. I had the pleasure of meeting him once, in his later years, and was sorely tempted to offer him an idea which might well have been conceived by himself: a song about a publican whom the singer had known and revered, who was now dead, whose business was carried on by his son, Ben, an excellent young man, —'But 'e'll never be the man 'is Father woz'. The chorus was to be something of this sort:

(*Sung*) 'I drops in to see young Ben
In 'is tap-room now an' then,
And I likes to see 'im gettin' on becoz
'E's got pluck and 'e's got brains,
And 'e takes no end o' pains,
But—'e'll never be the man 'is Father woz.'

But nothing so irks a creative artist as to be offered an idea, good or bad. And I did not irk Chevalier.

A man who introduces into an art-form a new style of his own has usually to pay a high price for having done so. Imitators crop up on all sides, cheapening his effects. This price Chevalier did not have to pay. He escaped in virtue of being partly French. His manner and method were inimitable in our rough island Halls. Singers of coster songs began to abound but they were thoroughly native and traditional. Gus Elen defied the conventions only by the extreme, the almost desperate glumness of his demeanour, and the bitterness of what he had to say, on a stage where cheeriness against all odds was ever the resounding key-note. Immensely acrid was the spirit of his ''E Dunno where 'e Are' and of his 'Well, it's a Grite Big Shime'; but even these were mild in comparison with the withering pessimism of a later song of his. Often in reading the work of some of those younger poets whom I have mentioned I am reminded of that other famous song, 'Wot's the good of ennyfink? Why, nuffink!'

Very different was the philosophy of Dan Leno. Fate had not smiled on him, his path was a hard one, he was beset by carking troubles and anxieties, he was all but at his wits' end, the shadow of the workhouse loomed, but there was in his little breast a passion of endurance, and a constant fount of hope, that nothing could subdue. His meagre face was writhen with care, but the gleam in his eyes proclaimed him undefeatable. He never asked for sympathy: he had too much of Cockney pride to do that; but the moment he appeared on the stage our hearts were all his. Nature had made him somehow irresistible. Nor do I remember any one so abundant in drollery of patter. He was, by the way, the inaugurator of patter. In his later years he hardly sang at all. There was just a perfunctory gabble of a stanza and a chorus, and the rest was a welter of the spoken word—and of imaginative genius.

He used to appear yearly in the Drury Lane pantomime, with the enormous Herbert Campbell as foil to him. But there he was wasted. Team-work nullified him. He could shine only in detachment. Besides, Drury Lane was too big for anybody but Herbert Campbell; and for him, it seemed to me, any Music Hall was too small. But I was very fond of him, that Boanergetic interpreter of the old tradition, with Mr. James Fawn as his only peer or rival. Physically somewhat less great than these two, Mr. Charles Godfrey had a wider range. He could be heroic as well as comic; and he abounded also in deep sentiment. 'After the Ball' is indeed a classic; but alas, as I found some years ago in a modern song book, the text has been corrupted, to suit tastes less naïve than ours were. The unsophisticated syntax of what Godfrey sang in his baggy dress-suit has been wantonly changed. No doubt you know the opening words of the present version. But what Godfrey gave us was

(*Sung*) 'Came a small maiden,
Climbed on my knees,
"Tell me a story,
Do, Uncle, please!"
"Tell you a story?
What shall I tell?
Tales about giants?
Or in the dell?"
After the Ball was over,
After the'——

and so on. But 'Tales about giants? Or in the dell?' That's the thing to remember and cherish.

Mr. Harry Freeman, dear man, sounded no depths, and scaled no heights of sentiment, and indeed had no pretensions of any kind, except a thorough knowledge of his business, which was the singing of songs about Beer, about the Lodger, about being had up before the Beak, about the Missus, about the sea-side, and all the other safest and surest themes. He never surprised one. He never disappointed one. He outstood in virtue of being a perfect symbol and emblem of the average. I delighted in him deeply. I think he had a steadying influence on me. To this day, whenever I am over-excited, or am tempted to take some unusual and unwise course, I think of Harry Freeman.

A saliently sharp antithesis to him was R. G. Knowles, surnamed 'The Very Peculiar American Comedian'. Nothing restful, everything peculiar, about *him*! He alone had a 'signature tune'. He was the inventor of that asset. The opening bars of Mendelssohn's Wedding March were played as he rushed on from the wings, hoarsely ejaculating 'I've only a moment to linger with you': a tall man with a rather scholarly face, wearing a very shabby frock-coat, an open collar, and not very white duck trousers, much frayed at the heels of very large old boots; also an opera-hat, flat-brimmed and tilted far back from the brow. He spoke rather huskily, with a strong native twang, at the rate of about ten words to the second. I tremble to think how many anecdotes he must always have uttered before he broke into a brief song and rushed away to linger for a moment with an audience in one of the other Halls. From some of his anecdotes one gathered that he was no prude. But there one wronged him. Some years ago my dear friend William Archer, the famous dramatic critic, and introducer of Ibsen to our shores, told me that he had recently met, travelling in India, a man of whom I probably knew a good deal, R. G. Knowles, a Music Hall performer. 'He told me,' said Archer, 'that he had definitely retired from the Music Halls; and I asked him why. He said that the tone of them had fallen to a very low level: there was so much that was ob-jectionable. He said, "Mr. Archer, in *my* turns there was never anything ob-jectionable. Sudge-estive–*yes.*"'

I am not in a position to deny that ob-jection-ability may have supervened. I had ceased to attend the Halls because the virus of 'Variety' had come creeping in: conjurors, performing elephants, tramp-bicyclists, lightning calculators, and so on, and so forth. The magic had fled–the dear old magic of the unity –the monotony, if you will–of song after song after song, good, bad, and indifferent, but all fusing one with another and cumulatively instilling a sense of deep beatitude–a strange sweet foretaste of Nirvana.

I often wondered, in the old Tivoli and elsewhere, who wrote the common ruck of the songs I was listening to, and what the writers bought one half so precious as the wares they sold. As to their tariff, I once had a queer little sidelight on that in a newspaper report of a case in the County Court at Hastings. The defendant stated that he earned his living by writing the words and music for Music Hall songs. He was asked by the Judge how much he earned in the course of a year. He replied promptly, 'Three hundred and sixty-five pounds.' And then, the Judge being astonished at such exactitude, he explained that he was paid one pound for every song, and wrote one every day.

I should have liked to learn more about him. That he was not of the straitest sect of Sabbatarians is obvious. For the rest, what manner of man was he? Was he entirely a creature of habit? Or had he sometimes to plod without aid from his Muse, while at other times she showered inspiration on him? Was it in the comic or in the sentimental vein that he was happier? And was he a discerning judge of his own work? For aught I know, he may have written and composed 'Daisy, Daisy, Give me your Answer True'. On the evening of that day, did he say to himself, 'Not marble nor the gilded monuments of princes shall outlive this powerful rhyme'? And this question leads to another. Why, exactly, has 'Daisy, Daisy' triumphed perennially, holding her ground against all comers? There is a reason for everything in this world, there is a solution of every mystery. And, with your co-operation, I should like to—but time forbids. I should like also to have said a great deal about Marie Lloyd, whose funeral was less impressive only than that of the great Duke of Wellington; about Little Tich, who took Paris by storm; about Vesta Tilley and Mark Sheridan; also about Miss Ada Reeve, and about Mr. George Robey. To her, and to him, and to the shades of those others, I apologise for my silence. The work of all of them gave me great delight in my youth. Perhaps you will blame me for having spent so much of my time in Music Halls, so frivolously, when I should have been sticking to my books, burning the midnight oil and compassing the larger latitude. But I am impenitent. I am inclined to think, indeed I have always thought, that a young man who desires to know all that in all ages and in all lands has been thought by the best minds, and wishes to make a synthesis of all those thoughts for the future benefit of mankind, is laying up for himself a very miserable old age.

Good night, childrenn. . . everywhhere.

ADVERTISEMENTS

(1942)

ADVERTISEMENTS

(Sunday evening, September 18th, 1942.)

Ladies and Gentlemen,—I am afraid my subject is rather an exciting one; and as I don't like excitement I shall approach it in a gentle, timid, round-about way. I am all for a quiet life. That is a deplorable confession, I suppose. I remember that many people were irritated and reproachful when, as a youngish man, I wrote in some newspaper, or in some book, that my ideal of happiness was 'a four-post bed in a field of poppies and mandragora'. London, when I wrote those words, was not so large a city as it has since become, but it was too large, and too civic, for my taste, and great always was my pleasure in getting away from it, for a while, whenever I could: away from the hustle and the jostle that ought to have been so congenial to me.

In 1910, when I was thirty-seven years old, I did altogether get away from it, to a little house on a coast-road of the Gulf of Genoa. A very quiet coast-road, traversed mostly by rustic carts and horses; a road on which a motor-car created excitement; a road on which little children ran races during a great part of the day. But a foreign country in war time—however friendly to one's cause—is an uncomforting place to be in. One wants to be where the English language is spoken, and English thoughts and feelings are expressed. Early in 1915 I was back in England, for rather more than the duration of what we ingenuously called the Great War. In the years that followed, considerable strides were being made along the aforesaid coast-road towards modern civilisation. The road itself was magnificently asphalted from side to side; the carts and horses were fewer than before; but great plenty of motor-cars and motor-bicycles more than atoned for this fewness; and the heartiness of their hooting and of their mostly open exhausts was a great improvement on the cries of those little boys and little girls who had been wont to run races, and could no longer do so . . . I wish, Ladies and Gentlemen, I could cure myself of the habit of speaking ironically. I should so like to express myself in a quite straightforward manner. But perhaps it's as well that I can't; for, if I could, my language might be over-strong for Sunday evening.

It is now four years since the darkening omens of another war brought me once more to England. Since then London has become a far quieter city, by day and by night, than it was in my youth, and an infinitely quieter one than it presently became; and now, when I come up to it from the country, I do not experience the shock with which it used to assail me. And I should feel thankful for the change if the reason for it were not so tragic a one. Or should I? A quiet capital city is a contradiction in terms. It is a thing uncanny, spectral. London is quiet for the first time in its history. I imagine that it never was noisier than in the seething days of the Elizabethans. In the eighteenth century life had become more or less canalised, the social structure had taken rigid shape. But Horace Walpole and the characters in 'The School for Scandal'—barring Charles Surface—were not typical of the time. It was rather Charles's time than Joseph's or Horace's: a robust and loud time. The Regency was an age of din, and the din did not immediately die down in Early Victorian times. It was modified only later by the coming in of the great new middle class, a class that was not, like the nobility and the mob, sure of itself. This slight lull ceased in the Edvardian Era—an Era which began many years before the death of Queen Victoria and lasted for four years after King Edward's death; an Era that was in its social manifestations very like to the Second Empire in France. Perhaps some young man who is listening to me has often thought he would like to have lived in Edvardian Days. I myself, when I was young, had a hankering after the Second Empire. I never realised that it was here and now—and I not enjoying it. Imagination is a great painter and gilder, is she not?

Of London in the period between the last war and this one I saw little; but I gather from what I have heard and read—from things said and written by quite good-natured, non-censorious people—that it is not a period of which one has great reason to feel, on the whole, proud. What I saw of it for myself seemed to me a distinctly inferior imitation of the Edvardian model. That model had not been altogether without grace. It assuredly had not lacked gusto. These qualities seemed to me rather lacking in the revival. But the noisiness was undeniably, I thought, greater. And the kind of noisiness that had increased more than any other was that visible kind which is especially unbeloved by me. There had been an horrific increase in the volume, the torrential spate and flood of—advertisements.

Those waters have now, of course, subsided

very much; they are comparatively a trickle. But I presume that after this war, if economic conditions permit, they will rise again in all their diluvian and submersive strength. Even now they are no mere trickle as compared with what they were in my childhood. And I confess to a fondness for the memory of those which found their way into my nursery. There was a fruit-salt of which I have since been told by experts that the proprietor was the Father of Modern Advertising. If indeed he was so, he, that dear old quiet man, builded greater than he knew. There was nothing startling, nothing arresting in his writings. They weren't even terse. They were by way of being prolix, and were interspersed with quotations from the Old Testament, and with references to anything that came into his head; and they were printed in very small, closely set, unassuming type. But I read them carefully, with all the pride of one who had but lately learned to read. And my fancy was always engaged by the accompanying rather smudgy wood-cut at the top of the column. I clearly remember the look of radiant well-being which not even the smudginess could disguise on the faces of the grandfather, the grandmother, the mother, the father and the children seated round a lamp-lit table with a turkey or a plum-pudding—or was it both?—in the midst of them. And there was a similar family eating its Christmas dinner out of doors, in the rays of the sun, in Australia. This struck a deep geographical chord of wonder in my little breast. Somewhat later, a wonderful soap swam into my ken. Sir John Millais had painted a great picture of a little boy with golden curls and a green velveteen suit, and upturned eyes, blowing bubbles; and this picture had been acquired by the vendor of the soap and widely reproduced on the soap's behalf. My elders, in those pre-historic days, wondered that Sir John should have authorised this use of his great gifts. And they were shocked, too, that the beautiful young Mrs. Langtry had for the soap's sake allowed engravings of a photograph of herself to be sown broadcast in the Press, with the admonition 'For look you, she is fair as a lily!' Mrs. Weldon, the famous litigant, had gone even further. Her portrait was subscribed by her, 'I am forty-seven, but my complexion is seventeen.' I wonder what my elders would think of those perfectly well-brought-up and non-litigious young ladies of rank and fashion who nowadays let their photographs be reproduced in favour of some unguent used by them and ecstatically praised by them, with an accompanying diagram of their features and a laudatory description of each feature by the unguentarian?

Only fools, of course, would accuse these young ladies of advertising themselves. They passionately believe in this or that balm and cannot but testify to the faith that is in them. But fools are not few in this world, and I rather wish the young ladies belonged to some guild that forbade its members to do anything that might be misconstrued as a desire for personal publicity. There is such a guild for doctors, another for barristers, another for stockbrokers, as we all know. Perhaps in course of time the Medical Council and the Bar Council and the Committee of the Stock Exchange will be broader-minded and more indulgent—who knows? Meanwhile their members are implacably debarred from advertising in the Press, and never do so. And yet, no, even as I speak these words, I remember—or rather even as I wrote these words to be read to you I remembered—an advertisement by a doctor, a very concise and therefore not expensive one, that caught my eye many years ago in *The Church Times*: 'Medical Man in Cheltenham can accommodate one female resident patient. Epileptic Churchwoman preferred.' This pleased me much; and of course there was nothing in it that could pain the Medical Council. The doctor did not give his name —gave merely his initials and 'Box' such and such a number; and he promised no cure at all. But perhaps he was the thin end of the wedge?

To these 'Want' advertisements, as I think they are called, to these spontaneous cries from the heart, I have no objection at all. It is the 'You *do* want, and woe betide if you don't get' ones that bore me to death. We are taught to believe that the outcriers are entirely altruistic men. Some years ago there was held at Wembley an International Advertising Convention, which lasted for three days or so. I was not present, but the speeches made at it were very fully reported in all the organs of the daily press. And I gathered that the Advertisers were very noble fellows indeed. They were spending themselves in what they called Service. The hall in which they met was adorned with strenuously edifying slogans: 'All for Each, and Each for All' is the one that I best remember. I gathered that these proprietors and these agents of theirs were not 'out', as they would have said, to make a good deal of money. Their aim, their incentive was just to serve you and me, to irradiate our darkness and give us full and happy lives. They spoke not as tradesmen; they spake as Crusaders, as Knights of the Holy Grail. I rather wondered they hadn't had a marching song composed for them. They ought to have come tramping from Wembley to London, four abreast, under flying banners, chanting a song with that almost sacred refrain: 'All for Each, and Each for All'. I am sorry to say that I presently struck a jarring note. I was having an exhibition of caricatures at the Leicester Galleries; and one of these, hung in the middle of one of the walls, was a group of strong, stout, square-jawed business men, with hands piously folded and brass haloes attached to their heads, and with a very rude inscription by me beneath them. I have often wondered who bought the nefarious thing. I am sorry to say that on the opening day it was one of the first drawings sold. It was described in two papers, *The Manchester Guardian* and *The Saturday Review*: the others drew over it the veil of pained silence.

Who was it—Lord Macaulay, I think—who first called the Press the Fourth Estate of the Realm? The advertisers are now certainly the Fifth. 'As you are strong', I venture to say to them, 'be merciful. Do try not to be quite so strong here as you are in, for instance, America.' I have seen American weekly and monthly magazines in which at first glance it isn't easy to find anything *but* advertisements. All the rest is printed in disjected fragments. An essay or a story begins briefly, say, on page 20, and then you must turn to page 33, and thence to page 47, amidst the glare and blare of things for sale. And in the London daily papers how much less space than of yore can be spared, could even before the war be spared, for consideration of the arts of literature, drama, painting, music—or even for the utterances of senators. Of course the advertisers are not really to blame, nor are the editors. The mischief is due to the enormous increase in the cost of producing a newspaper. The cost of book-production has, I suppose, gone up not less hideously. But so far the pages of novels or poems, of essays or biographies, have not been interspersed by their publishers with pæans on the various competing brands of whisky and millinery and cigarettes. Perhaps, after we have won the war, not even *this* mercy will be vouchsafed to us. Meanwhile, if I were endowed with wealth, I should start a great advertising campaign in all the principal newspapers. The advertisements would consist of one short sentence, printed in huge block letters—a sentence that I once heard spoken by a husband to a wife: 'My dear, nothing in this world is worth buying'. But of course I should alter 'my dear' to 'my dears'.

And now for a matter which agitates me far more than the effect that advertisements have on newspapers. Though newspapers without advertisements could not nowadays survive, I see no reason for believing that without this support the streets and squares of our cities, and the roads and hills and valleys of our countryside, would presently disappear. On the contrary, they are rather by way of disappearing already behind the insistences on what we ought to purchase. Beautiful architecture and beautiful scenery are things far more important to the soul of man than even the best newspaper. So too is the sky, surely; especially the sky by night. But the advertisers are creatures of the night as well as of the day. Some years ago, a clever man invented a device by which illuminated advertisements could be inscribed upon the sky by night and would remain fixed there for a fairly long time. The sanction of Parliament was somehow necessary to the execution of this plan. There was strong opposition to it from many quarters, certainly from all the best ones. But the Bill, with some slight modification, was passed by both Houses. That beautiful quarter of London, the Adelphi, had recently been handed over by them for demolition and for skyscrapers. Why *shouldn't* the sky be scraped? And why shouldn't it have advertisements scrawled on it? Is this a free country, or is it not? What right have its rulers to prevent *anybody* from making money wherever he sees a chance of doing so? To hinder him, thought the majority of Lords and Commons, would be un-English. Some of them perhaps went even further, and thought that it wouldn't be cricket.

But the invention seems not to have fulfilled its dreadful promise. So far as I know, the space between us and the stars remained unmolested, and all was well. And now, during this war we can further be glad of one thing: that London by night is not vulgarised and debased by those loathsome red-hot-coal illuminations, appearing and clumsily spelling themselves out and disappearing and re-appearing on the copings and façades of buildings. If such things must be, let them be done with some semblance of taste and fancy. Many of you will have seen and rather liked, in this and that foreign city, those inscriptions in neon light on the frontages of shops by night: inscriptions done in graceful, fluent lettering, and in pleasant tints—primrose, or pale pink, or lavender. But in the average foreign country there is a Ministry of Fine Arts, and to that Ministry all such spectacular advertisements must be submitted, and by it approved. We ourselves nowadays have a Ministry of almost everything. Some day perhaps we shall have one of Fine Arts? But I fancy we shan't ever have one, and that if we had one it would quake in abject terror of any vested interests.

And on that note of mild pessimism, Ladies and Gentlemen, I will bid you good night. I told you at the outset that my subject was an exciting one. If I haven't made it seem so to you, don't accuse me of breach of faith. I didn't promise you that *I* wasn't going to be rather dull. Besides, you must remember that not one of you has been listening to me for his or her own sake, for his or her own gratification. You have been listening All for Each, and Each for All.

PLAYGOING

(1945)

PLAYGOING

(*Sunday evening, October 8th, 1945.*)

Ladies and Gentlemen,–The title I have chosen for this soliloquy has rather an old-world flavour. But I myself am one of the relics of an older, an easier and more pleasant and yet a more formal world than this one, and my lips were loth to frame the modern equivalent, 'Doing a Show'. I might have said, 'Going to the Play', which was a familiar phrase in the Victorian and Edvardian eras. Familiar but strange. The use of the definite article was so very indefinitive. Going to *what* play? There was always more than one; though certainly plays were fewer, and theatres fewer, and we had only two or three dramatists—only two or three, I mean, who were alive and also worth mentioning. In fact, for better or worse, things were very different. Let me maunder over some of the differences.

Actors and actresses were certainly regarded with far greater interest than they are nowadays. The outstanding ones inspired something deeper than interest. It was with excitement, with wonder and with reverence, with something akin even to hysteria, that they were gazed upon. Some of the younger of you listeners would, no doubt, if they could, interrupt me at this point by asking, 'But surely you don't mean, do you, that our parents and grandparents were affected by them as we are by cinema stars?' I would assure you that those idols of ours were even more ardently worshipped than are yours. Yours, after all, are but images of idols, mere shadows of glory. Those others were their own selves, creatures of flesh and blood, there, before our eyes. They were performing in our presence. And of our presence they were aware. Even we, in all our humility, acted as stimulants to them. The magnetism diffused by them across the footlights was in some degree our own doing. You, on the other hand, have nothing to do with the performances of which you witness the result. Those performances—or rather those innumerable rehearsals—took place in some far-away gaunt studio in Hollywood or elsewhere, months ago. Those moving shadows will be making identically the same movements at the next performance, or rather at the next record; and in the inflexions of those voices enlarged and preserved for you there by machinery not one cadence will be altered. Thus the theatre has certain advantages over the cinema, and in virtue of them will continue to survive. But the thrill of it is not quite what it was in my young days.

In those piping days of yore, there was in playgoing a spice of adventure, of audacity. The theatre was frowned on by quite a large part of the community. The Nonconformist Churches were, without exception, dead against it. Ministers of even the Church of England were very dubious about it and never attended it. Players were no longer regarded in the eighteen-eighties and 'nineties as rogues and vagabonds, but the old Puritan prejudice against them still flourished. Not long ago I came across an excellent little book published in the 'sixties, entitled *A Manual for Chess Players*. It had as preface a very erudite history of the game, in the course of which occurred these words: 'Chess has throughout the ages been the favourite pastime of all sorts and conditions of men, from Popes and Emperors to actors and dustmen.' And here is another straw to show that the wind was still blowing briskly that way even in the 'eighties. A small boy, a son of that great actress, Mrs. Kendal, on his first day at a preparatory school in London, was asked by an elder boy, 'Your mother's an actress, isn't she?' He replied with spirit, 'If you say that again, I'll knock you down.' I remember, too, that at the public school to which I was admitted in 1885 none of the boys, though my elder brother, Herbert Beerbohm Tree, was already a well-known actor, ever referred to our brotherhood. It was only in 1887, when Herbert became an actor-manager, that the silence was broken, that the subject ceased to be a delicate one. An actor-*manager* could be mentioned quite frankly, and even with awe.

Well, the days of the actor-manager are past. No doubt he was not a faultless institution. But he was an impressive and exciting one. There he was, in his own theatre, and giving to that theatre a definite individuality of its own. It was not merely a building, it was a kind of temple, with its own special brand of worshippers. First nights were thrilling, throbbing occasions. People had come not so much to see a mere play as to see a play with their idol in it. They hoped the play would be a success for *his* sake. If it seemed to them a failure the pit and gallery booed the author for having betrayed their idol. They were in no mood to stand any nonsense from an author. Many of them had been sitting on camp-stools, or standing for hours and hours outside the theatre, patiently, smilingly, devotedly. Some of them even were quick to resent in one of the characters of the play any lack of right feeling for the leading man. I remember the first night of a play written for Mr. Lewis Waller—a play in which he was an important Anglo-Indian soldier, in a white uniform and in command of a province. In the second act there came to him an evil native with a petition of a kind that Mr. Waller could not grant. The native produced a pistol and fired it at him. I was in the back row of the stalls, and was almost deafened by a young lady who, in the front row of the pit, screamed 'How *dare* he?'

I remember also a first night in which that excellent romantic actor, in his speech before the curtain, thanked the audience for their 'loyalty' to him. And indeed that word was not inappropriate. Actor-managers were kings, in their fashion—in the English, the constitutional fashion: not autocrats in danger of their lives. In the daytime they drove about unguarded in hansom cabs—or even walked, taking the pavement with as easy a grace as that with which they took the boards.

They are gone. They have been replaced by theatrical syndicates. Are you thrilled when you see a syndicate sauntering down Piccadilly or driving down it in a *char-à-banc*? Is your pulse quickened by the thought of the awful financial risks taken by these brave fellows? Do you pray that their box-offices will be for ever besieged? I fear you are coldly concerned with the mere question whether the play they are running is a good one, worthy of your respect. Even if they themselves were playing the male parts in it the sight of them out in the open air would not deeply stir you. The play, not so much the players nowadays, is what you are really keen on. 'The play's the thing.'

And it is, on the whole, a better thing than it used to be. In my very young days it was mostly something adapted from the French, and had suffered greatly in the Channel crossing. Henry Arthur Jones and Arthur Wing Pinero were almost alone in having both a sense of the theatre and a sense of the realities of life. And the Americans gave us no help. Mr. Augustin Daly's farces were then her sole export, and not at all a good one. America was very grateful for the imports she got from us. Meanwhile in Norway a great grim dramaturgist was every morning at his desk, unresting but unhurrying, giving to his compatriots one play every two years. And in England there was a Scotsman who knew the Norwegian tongue and translated the biennial achievement. Towards the end of the 'eighties he even managed to get the latest of those achievements produced precariously in some small theatre in London. The dramatic critics of that time were a less sophisticated race than the present one. They were a race of cheerful hacks. They did not see eye to eye with their argute Scottish colleague, William Archer, on the merits of 'A Doll's House'. Even A. B. Walkley, though he of course recognised the magnitude of Ibsen, found Ibsen rather rebarbative; and Bernard Shaw, though promptly Ibsenite, had not yet become a dramatic critic. The Ibsen movement became more mobile later on, when a very dynamic and fervent little Dutchman, J. T. Grein, who was not at all content with being 'something in the City' and being also Consul for Bolivia, rushed in, founded The Independent Theatre and produced 'Ghosts'. And lo, there was a terrific outcry against

Ibsen. But there was also an earnest outcry *for* him, raised by people who had hitherto rather disdained the theatre. There was so much to be said for the Ibsen method—for the stage as just a three-walled room, with some people in it talking in a perfectly natural manner; not doing much, but thinking and feeling deeply; and illustrating some idea, and presenting some problem or other; and with no prospect of that happy ending to which the public was accustomed. And presently, under the Ibsen influence, Mr. Pinero wrote 'The Second Mrs. Tanqueray'. I am told that it seems very artificial nowadays; but it seemed dreadfully, delightfully true to nature then. And anon came the Stage Society, with performances of earlier and later plays by Ibsen, and of plays by other more or less grim foreigners, and of a play or two already by Bernard Shaw. And very superior young men who had never thought of writing for the theatre began to do so, not without some measure of devious success. And in course of time it befell that Shaw became actually popular. Harley Granville-Barker, allied with Mr. Vedrenne, had brilliantly established himself in the Court Theatre, and it was there that 'Man and Superman' was produced. Someone told King Edward that it was a play he ought to see. One night he came and saw it. Then came all rank and fashion to see it. And the bourgeoisie came to see *them*. And incidentally both the seers and the seen discovered that Shaw was really a most delightful person.

At that time I was a dramatic critic, and very angry that not all the theatres in London were given over to intellectual drama. I was still in that mood when, thirty-five years ago, I retired from dramatic criticism, and left London, and ceased to go to theatres. My nature then mellowed. I became tolerant of whatever might be going on behind my back. But I gathered from the newspapers that my former colleagues, especially the younger ones, seemed to grow more and more distressed about things, and I remember that in about 1912 I composed in my head a drinking-song for them. I didn't send it to them, for I was afraid they might think the metre too cheerful. It ran as follows:

In days of yore the Drama throve
  Within our storm-bound coasts,
The Independent Theatre gave
  Performances of 'Ghosts',
Death and disease, disaster
  And downfall were our joy,
The fun flew fast and faster
  While Ibsen was our Master
And Grein was a bright Dutch boy, my boys,
  And Grein was a bright Dutch boy.

The Future of the Drama
  Was our theme day in, day out,
Pinero was most sanguine,
  Henry Arthur had no doubt.
'On, on!' cried William Archer,
  And no man was less coy
Than Shaw, that spring-heel'd marcher
  In *any* new deparcher,
When Grein was a bright Dutch boy, my boys,
  When Grein was a bright Dutch boy.

The Movies moved not yet, my boys,
  Revues were not in view,
The present state of things was not
  Foreseen by me and you.

We sailed o'er seas uncharted
Of youth and faith and joy.
None cried 'Are we downhearted?'
In those dear days departed
When Grein was a bright Dutch boy, my boys.
When Grein was a bright Dutch boy.

For any man who has been and is no longer a dramatic critic there is a peculiar pleasure in play-going, even if the play be a bad one, and even if the theatre be one of those austere, bleak, neutral-tinted, ferro-concrete tabernacles which the modern architect and his upholsterer seem to think preferable to such genial places as the Haymarket or the St. James's, and even if the players be seeming to forget that the room they are in is only a *three*-walled one, and that we are come to hear what they have to say. For such a man there is the bliss of knowing that he need not write one line about what is going on—need not be anxiously on the look-out for some point of view from which he could compose an article which readers would think clever and would enjoy. Oh yes, I assure you I am very mellow. If the bad old times, and with them the bad old tricks (the 'soliloquy', the 'aside', and so on) came in again, I think I should rather welcome them, for old sake's sake. And if intellectual ideas were to vanish from the boards I am not sure that my heart would break. Indeed, I have a sort of feeling that one can appreciate ideas, is more susceptible to them and better able to grapple with them, when they are set forth in a book that one is reading by one's own fireside than when they are mooted to an auditorium. One can pause, can linger, can perpend. I have a notion that the drama is, after all, essentially a vehicle for action (for drama, as the Greeks quite frankly called it), is essentially, or at least mainly, a thing to cause the excitement of pity and awe, or of terror, or of laughter, rather than to stimulate one's ratiocinative faculties. The theatre, I would say, is a place for thrills. You may, of course, be thrilled at your fireside by a book of philosophy or of history. You are still more likely to be so by a fine work of fiction. But the characters in a novel are not there before your very eyes, saying and doing things in your very presence. The novelist's power to startle you, or to hold you in breathless suspense, is a slight one in comparison with the dramatist's. All the vividest of my memories of the theatre are memories of stark 'situations'—the appearance of the Ghost on the battlements at Elsinore; or the knocking at the gate while Duncan is murdered, and the repetition of that knocking; or the screen with Lady Teazle behind it, and the fall of that screen; or, in plays of later date, 'Who are you?'—'HAWKSHAW, the detective!'—CURTAIN. Or 'Disguise is useless! You are MACARI!' Or, in Oscar Wilde's classic farce, the appearance of Algernon, in deepest mourning, at the garden gate, to announce the death of his figmentary brother.

Is this a Philistine standpoint? Well, I have no time to defend myself, and I fear you are glad that I haven't. I fear that you, Ladies and Gentlemen, have *not* been thrilled by *me* at your firesides, and are yearning for the next item on the programme: BARCAROLLE. And at this moment the Barcarollists are straining at the leash. Good night.

A NOTE ON THE EINSTEIN THEORY

(1923)

A NOTE ON THE EINSTEIN THEORY

(*1923.*)

It is said that there are, besides Dr. Einstein himself, only two men who can claim to have grasped the Theory in full. I cannot claim to be either of these. But I do know a good thing when I see it; and here is a thing that is excellent in its kind—romantically excellent in a kind that is itself high. When I think of rays being deflected by gravity, and of parallel lines at long last converging so that there isn't perhaps, after all, any such thing as Infinity, I draw a very deep breath indeed. The attempt to conceive Infinity had always been quite arduous enough for me. But to imagine the absence of it; to feel that perhaps we and all the stars beyond our ken are somehow cosily (though awfully) closed in by certain curves beyond which is nothing; and to convince myself, by the way, that this exterior nothing is not (in virtue of *being* nothing) something, and therefore . . . but I lose the thread.

Enough that I never lose the thrill. It excites, it charms me to think of elderly great mathematicians of this and that nation packing their portmanteaus whenever there is to be a solar eclipse, and travelling over land and sea to the Lick Observatory, or to some hardly accessible mountain-top in Kamchatka, and there testing, to the best of their power, the soundness or unsoundness of the tremendous Theory. So far, the weather has not been very favourable to these undertakings. Nature, who is proud and secretive, has opposed many clouds to the batteries of telescopes. But she has had only a partial success, it seems. Some observations have been more or less clearly made, some conclusions more or less clearly drawn. And these more or less clearly point to the likelihood that what Dr. Einstein in his humdrum home evolved from his inner consciousness is all delightfully correct.

But is the British public delighted? It gives no sign of being so. Its newspapers did at the first news of Einstein's existence try, very honourably, to excite it about Einstein and even about his work. It would *not* be excited. Strange! The tamest batting of Hertfordshire *v.* Australia, the feeblest goal-keeping of Wormwood Scrubbs *v.* Hornsey Rise, the lightest word that falls from the lips of the least accomplished negro boxer, are better 'copy' than any challenge to our notion of the Cosmos. This is all the stranger because the public is not careless of other things than Sport. Its passionate interest in archæology, for instance, rose to boiling-point, only the other day: it could *not* hear too much about the tomb of Tutankhamen, nor tire of debating whether or not the bones of that king might rightly be disturbed. Why never a word as to the disturbance of our belief that parallel lines can nowhere converge? I haven't grudged Tutankhamen the renewal and immense enlargement of the fame he once had. I have but deplored the huge cold shoulder turned on the living Einstein.

Newton, no greater an innovator than he, is popular enough. Everybody knows something about Gravitation—and all about the apple. Perhaps if Newton had not mentioned that apple, he too would be generally ignored. It is a great advantage for a discoverer to have been inspired by some homely little incident. Newton and the apple, Copernicus and the whipping-top, James Watt and the kettle. But Einstein and——? Poor Einstein!

Men of his magnitude are not avid of popularity? True; but this does not mean that popularity would be disagreeable to them. When the newspapers were trying to make Relativity a household word, I read an account of Einstein, written by one who knew him, and enhanced by a photograph of him. A very human person, I gathered; far from stand-off-ish; a player of the fiddle; the constant smoker of a large pipe; a genial, though thoughtful, critic of current things. I liked his views on education. Why all this forcing of a child's memory? Memory—a matter of little moment. Let the child be taught to see, and to think, for itself. And let every child be taught a trade. And 'after all,' said Einstein, dismissing tuition, 'the best thing in the world is a happy face.' It was clear from the photograph that his own face was a happy one. But I discerned in it a certain wistfulness, too—the wistfulness of a thorough good fellow whose work somehow repels the attention of that good fellow, the average man. My heart went out to him. I wished I could help him. And now, I think, I can. Hark!

Yesterday afternoon I was walking on the coast-road from Rapallo to Zoagli when I saw approaching in the distance a man of strenuous gait, and of aspect neither Italian nor English. His brow was bare to the breeze; and as he drew near I perceived the brow to be a fine one; and as he drew nearer still I perceived the face to be a very happy one—with just a hint in it of wistfulness, which, however, vanished at my words, 'Dr. Einstein, I presume?' He clapped a cordial hand on my shoulder; he treated me as an old friend, as a brother, and insisted that we should sit together on the low wall that divides the road from the cliff. Presently—after he had praised the sun and the sea, and had expressed an ardent sympathy with Fascismo, and with Socialismo, no less—I said to him, 'Master (if one who is not a disciple may so address you), tell me: What was it that first put you on the track of the tremendous Theory?' He knitted his fine brow, saying that his memory was not a very good one; but after a while he remembered, and spoke to me as follows:

'One winter's evening, after a hard day's work, I was sitting by my fireside—for I have an open fire in the English fashion, not a stove: I like to sit watching the happy faces in the coals—when my eye lighted on the tongs in the fender. Of course it had often lighted on them before; but this time it carried to my brain a message which my brain could not understand. "Here," I mused, "are two perfectly parallel lines. And yet, and yet, they meet at the extreme ends. How is that?" My friend Professor Schultz had promised to drop in and smoke a pipe with me that evening, and when he came I drew his attention to the phenomenon. He knelt down by the fender, pushed his spectacles up on to his forehead, gazed closely, and muttered, "Gott in Himmel—ja!" I asked him—for he is a very ready man—if he had any explanation to offer. He rose from his knees and sat down on a chair heavily, burying his head in his hands. Suddenly he sprang to his feet. "Einstein," he said, "I believe I have it! I believe that the iron-worker who made those bars must have heated them red-hot and then bent the ends towards each other." Dear old Schultz! Always so ready!—so shallow! I suppose I ought not to have laughed; but I did; and Schultz went out in some anger. It was dawn when I rose from the fireside. The fire had long ago burnt itself out, and I was stiff with cold. But my mind was all aglow with the basic principles of Relativismus.'

'The world,' I said quietly, 'shall hear of this, Dr. Einstein.'

FROM BLOOMSBURY TO BAYSWATER

(1940)

FROM BLOOMSBURY TO BAYSWATER

(*1940.*)

In August, 1935, it seemed that we might at any moment be at war with Italy, a country in which I had resided for many years. Accordingly I returned to the land of my birth and heart; and the stormy petrel, partly by chance, and partly for good reasons of economy, folded its wings in Bloomsbury, and was there for rather more than a year.

Tavistock Square is not so fine a place as Bedford Square or Brunswick Square; but it is (as you will already have guessed) a Square, and has therefore much to be said for it. Very greatly did I enjoy the charm of seeing through my two large windows on the ground-floor the gradual turn of the leaf, the yellowing and the browning of it, its fall, its wind-swept eddying along the road; and the austere nakedness of the great old trees, offering a distant view of the houses on the other side, and of the omnibuses that passed incessantly along that unhappy other side and blessedly couldn't be heard on ours; and in due time the clean snow upon the grass and upon the soot-black but noble branches; and later the small green buds that are so much stranger than on country trees; and gradually the disappearance of the inaudible omnibuses and of the windows of the unblest; and then again the yellowing and the browning, the falling and the eddying. It is in a city, surely, that the lover of Nature finds deepest pleasure in watching her old round of phases.

Nevertheless, he prefers the country; and I am sure that in the eighteenth century I should have wished to murder that Duke of Bedford who for purposes of pelf had his great house demolished, and his park and his fields innumerable built over by a bright young architect and surveyor. I should not have realised that the architecture was good. I should have taken its manner as a matter of course. The spaciousness and solidity and homely grandeur of it all, the generous width of its doors and door-steps and of its areas, would have won no word of praise from my pursed-up lips. Nor would the correspondingly generous width of the roads and of the pavements have surprised and mollified me. One lives and learns. One lives another century and a half and begins to appreciate.

In my youth Bloomsbury meant little to me. It didn't—it doesn't even now—appeal to the historic sense. Such places as St. James's and Westminster and Mayfair had always had shining inmates: such places were of the centre, and near the rose. Bloomsbury in its day was much favoured by eminent lawyers, and by their wives and families. And outside their courts lawyers mostly burn with but a dim light. Moreover, they had deserted Bloomsbury before I was born, leaving their houses to the letters of lodgings and to the keepers of boarding-houses, or even to emptiness and darkness, or even to disrepute. If Bloomsbury had vanished utterly, my young heart would not have mourned it. But now it *is* beginning to vanish little by little. Many of the Squares and Streets have been more or less vandalised. All of them are threatened. I gather that the arch-threatener is the University of London. I understand that there are no limits to its desire for expansion of that bleak, blank, hideous and already vast whited sepulchre which bears its name. Simultaneous tens of thousands of youths and maidens yet unborn will in the not so very far distant future be having their minds filled there and their souls starved there. Poor things! (And I'm sorry for the dons too.)

To them, perhaps, what may remain of the present Bloomsbury will have that historic interest which for us it lacks. They may say to one another, 'In that small brown house yonder, Henry Smith wrote his immortal "Snarls",' and 'In that one, Philip Robinson painted some of the most exquisitely unsightly of his dissignifications.' For of course, since 1918 or so, Bloomsbury has got into inverted commas, and has (though Philip Robinson will blame me for using the word) a meaning. It has become an intellectual centre, or, as it would call itself (for it is very Russian in its leanings), a focus of the intelligentsia. I myself am not *very* Russian, and to me the term 'intelligentsia' seems less modest and less apt than 'mental underworld'. Dostoievsky, their god, was a man of genius, certainly, and gave beautifully poignant expression to his spinelessness. But he is altogether alien to our rough island race; and laborious little imitations of his inspired maunderings cut no ice, and win scant patience from the average reader, even if they are contrived in all deep reverence to the memory of Karl Marx, and in fond though violent indigestion of the theories of Dr. Freud. But here I am presuming an average reader able to elucidate those tricksy snippets of dry prose in which the poetry of the West Central young is written. Here am I forgetting that intelligibility is as darkly frowned on by these young as are those stuffy old fads of the Victorian bourgeoisie, beauty, harmony, movement, development, and similar rot that had been handed down from the dark ages of Periclean Athens and had loathsomely imposed itself on generation after craven generation of the cloddish human race, and was seen through and discarded only as a result of the European War of 1914–1918.

Certainly that war was a bad time to be born in, and the subsequent years must have been unhappy ones to grow up in. I daresay that were I a young man of the period I too should be disgruntled. I was fortunate in the (almost pre-historic) date of my birth. Even so, however, I was foolish enough in my youth, as is the way of young men. But I wonder whether, if I were young now, I should be quite such a fool as to suppose that literary or graphic artists can advantageously forgo the influence of tradition and start with quite clean slates. The world has been going on for ever so long, with ever so many gifted people in it. Anything that is worth doing has been done frequently. Things hitherto undone should be given, I suspect, a wide berth. Let the young rise in revolt, from time to time, by all means. But, to be fruitful, their revolts must be, in another sense, from time to time: from the present to the past. In the nineteenth century there were two movements of importance; one of them a revolt from the formalism of the previous century, the other from the current fashions of academic art. But Romance was, after all, an old and familiar affair; nor were Giotto and his kind imaginary figures. The only novelty was the style in which the old ways were handled and developed and extended in the new period. The Impressionists? For the moment, I was forgetting them. But they are no snag. None of my Chelsea friends of the 'nineties supposed Manet to have been a phœnix. Steer and Sickert, MacColl and Will Rothenstein, were all vocally aware of kings before Agamemnon—Spanish, Italian, and other kings.

I wonder that the Chelsea of those days could have slipped my memory, so obvious is the contrast of it with the Bloomsbury of these!—so fresh and tonic was the air of it; so gay were the artists of that village (for village it still seemed to be) by the riverside. Why hasn't Bloomsbury a river?—a cheering, strong-flowing river, washing things away to the sea. I feel sure that even in the inter-bella period a river would have done Bloomsbury no end of good. Regent's Park is very airy, and isn't very far away from Bloomsbury; but it is a smug, urban expanse, and, such as it is, can be reached only by walking along the Euston Road, awfullest of thoroughfares, and is therefore valueless for the purpose of bracing up the spirits of the Bloomsburyites and giving them that lively faith in themselves and in their works which is just what, in my daily rovings around the district, and in my observings of the passers-by, they seemed to me to lack. The passers-by were never many. The inhabitants didn't seem to take much exercise. They seemed to be mostly at home and at work all day. And it may be that none of the young men and women who passed by me was a poet or a painter, or even a critic. But some of them, I thought, must be something of that kind. And I wished they would bear themselves more proudly. I did not demand of them defiance. I merely craved an air of young self-confidence—a pleasant touch of juvenile swagger. Their work was treated with deep respect by most of the elderly reviewers (terrified of not seeming abreast of the times). But they seemed to be not elated by the timorous eulogies that were heaped on them. Their eyes lacked lustre. Their cigarettes drooped almost vertically from between lips that never broke into a smile. And sometimes, I noted, they were wearing very muddy shoes though the sun had for several days been shining brilliantly. But there was one of them (and he a foreigner, I was told) who stood out distinctly from the rest: he was a tall, thin, keen-faced man with short side-whiskers; and he wore a kind of tam-o'-shanter, a brick-coloured cloak, a long robe to match, and a pair of sandals; and his brown hair fell to the back of his waist, and in windy weather streamed out behind him with immense vivacity. He attracted great attention always, and comment too, of course. The best comment on him that I overheard was made by one of two costermongers whom he had just passed by. 'Well, Bill,' said the one to the other, who was grinning widely, 'at any rate 'e's got more courage than wot *we*'ve got.'

These words, so typical of cockney wisdom and tolerance, impressed me deeply. And perhaps it was they that caused me, me too, to become courageous. I had read in letters to the press many hostile references to 'the Old School Tie', as a symbol of snobbish devotion to an individuality-crushing old horrid system, and had thought to myself, 'What nonsense!' It had never occurred to me to exercise my right to wear such a tie. But now, here, in the heart of Bloomsbury, I felt that I would belatedly do so, and I went to my hosier and ordered two Old Carthusian ties. Do you know the colours? They are three: bright crimson, salmon pink, and royal blue. They are dangerous to the appearance of even a quite young man. To that of an old man they are utterly disastrous. Nevertheless, I, without faltering, wore one of my pair until my sojourn in Bloomsbury came to its end.

This was in October, 1936. The Anglo-Italian horizon had cleared. I returned to my home in Italy. In August of the next year but one, that horizon was again dark. One didn't know at what moment Hitler might strike, nor whether Mussolini wouldn't strike with him. Behold me again upon this isle!—but, this time, in Bayswater, where, indeed, I had been born and had lived (barring school-terms) until I was sixteen. A touching picture. The return of the old native.

There, in Inverness Terrace, I abode for some months, remembering Bloomsbury, and marvelling how two districts with but a few miles between them could have inhabitants so immeasurably different.

Bayswater! Is there no magic for you, reader, in that name? There had been none in it for me. But I'm not at all sure that it won't be found graven on my heart—graven there by the feeble hand of Bloomsbury.

Is it the climate that makes the difference? Bayswater is on a higher lever, certainly. Or is it the soil? Bloomsbury, I am sure, is on clay, and Bayswater on gravel. Or is it the presence of Kensington Gardens? As is the river to Chelsea, so is (or are?) Kensington Gardens to Bayswater—exhilarating, purging, cobweb-preventing, spirit-of-village preserving.

Even in the darkest days of the autumnal crisis the mien of the inhabitants was suggestive of Merrie England. Swinging was their gait, bright were their eyes, clear their complexions, obviously high their spirits. The scene was Arcadian, the scene seemed vernal. The young women hadn't masked their faces with make-up nor plucked out their eyebrows, and weren't smoking, and were mostly wheeling perambulators with babies in them. The young men accompanying them seemed not to have a care in the world, and were mostly wearing Old School Ties. And the old people looked quite young. Time does not age the people of Bayswater.

OLD CARTHUSIAN MEMORIES

(1920)

OLD CARTHUSIAN MEMORIES

(*1920.*)

I am afraid I was never an Old Carthusian of the straitest sect. I remember that in my first term at Oxford (A.D. 1890) I did a drawing of Thomas Sutton, whose features had been so familiar to me during the past five years; and under it I wrote these three elegiac couplets :

FLORUIT innumeros Schola Carthusiana per annos,
Olim Londinii pessima pernicies.
FLORET in aerio jam condita vertice montis
Quingentosque docet tristitiam pueros.
FLOREBIT, nec non Plutonis regna manebunt.
Altera ut agnoscam sum memor alterius.

The drawing was a gross caricature of that grand old merchant, and the verses were an unpardonable libel on my views. I thought Charterhouse a very fine school really. I was very glad of having been there. But——no, I was *not* of the straitest sect. My delight in having been at Charterhouse was far greater than had been my delight in being there. I was well content to be where I was : in Oxford. I am well content to be where I am : in Rapallo. The straitest sect is never happy. It simply can't bear the thought of having left Charterhouse. After-life for it is one long anticlimax. It simply can't forget that goal which Gownboys kicked in that match against Hodgsonites.

It cherishes all the old jokes about Monsieur Petilleau. It remembers how prismatically in winter-time the morning sun used to glow through the east window of Chapel. It would gladly be liable to write out and show up a hundred lines or more for whatever fault it may commit. It recalls how splendidly Prescott mi. scored off old Judson about those decimals. It still vibrates with the thrill it felt on that Saturday evening when the Rifle Corps brought back the Ashburton Shield from Bisley for the fourth time running. The future leaves it cold. The present enchants it not at all. It sees even now the black eye that Simpson gave Thompson for calling him a rotter. And it dies with the word Adsum on its lips.

'C'est bien beau, cet amour qui est plus fort que la mort.' But is it not rather hard on a man's wife and children and friends? *Ought* he to walk backwards along the high-road of life, with his eyes ever yearningly fixed on the more and more distant spires of his old school? Carthusiana Domus—a beautiful phrase, yes. Let a boy at school regard his school as a home, if he can do so, by all means. But let him not be homesick for it ever after. I said that I was 'afraid' I did not belong to the straitest sect. That was not quite sincere. It was but an orator's device for conciliating his audience at the outset. I am very glad not to be of the straitest sect, and glad also that this sect is not (so far as I have been able to observe) a large one. Passionately retroverted Old Etonians are common enough in my experience; and I have known a great number of quite maudlin Old Wykehamists. But among Old Carthusians I have noted few cases of schoolsickness (that terrible scourge) in its more virulent forms. Perhaps the keenly bracing air of the Surrey hilltop tends to destroy in a lad's breast the germs of excessive sentiment. If Dr. Haig-Brown had been an ordinary, conservative, unimaginative man, saying, 'All's for the best in this best of all possible Greyfriars,' and had *not* led his flock forth (in 1872, wasn't it?) to those pastures above Godalming, perhaps we Old Carthusians would be less sanely romantic than we are. Climate does much. Architecture also, I think, does something. Charterhouse is very handsome. This epithet is not one which would leap to the lips of a man beholding Eton or Winchester—or Charterhouse in the City of London. Of such places no man would say, 'How well-adapted to the purpose in view! The very stones cry out "Efficiency"!' Those mouldering stones and discoloured bricks, all that decaying wood-work, strike no chord in the practical side of our nature. They do not seem anxious to satisfy us. They seem to be brooding over old memories. And we find ourselves brooding with them. Had Thomas Sutton had a roving eye and adventurous spirit, like Dr. Haig-Brown, and seen yonder hilltop, and climbed it, and said to his stonemasons, 'It is here that ye shall build,' then, I fancy again, there might be less sanity than there is in our Old Carthusian romanticism. I never see Charterhouse without reflecting how good for me were the five years I spent there. But I have not that unreasonable emotion which comes to me when I revisit Oxford. Oxford, too, was good for me, in its different way. Yet I do not think there of any gain I may have had therefrom. The practical side of my nature falls into abeyance. This happens also, to some extent, when I go to Greyfriars. I feel there rather as an American of English ancestry may be supposed to feel when he visits England: 'Here is the beautiful little old cradle of my race.' But the American has to reflect that he himself was never rocked in that cradle. He knows he has a strong American accent. In Greyfriars I feel that I have a strong Surrey accent, and only a rather remote kinship with Addison and Steele.

The good that those aforesaid five years did me——'isn't,' my young readers interrupt me, 'very clear to *us*.' I was about to say that had I been educated by a private tutor I should have become a prig and an egoist. 'But,' say my young readers, 'isn't that just what you *have* become?' To a certain extent, yes, perhaps. But I should be much worse if I hadn't been at Charterhouse. I am, moreover, much better than my young readers suppose. When the Editor of *The Carthusian* asks one to write some memories, it is difficult to avoid egoism. And I am not really priggish when I haven't a pen in my hand, believe me. The very fact that I foresaw your distaste for what I have written shows that I have a power of getting outside myself. That is a very useful power. And it is a power which a shy and sensitive and pensive little boy learns better at a public school than he could anywhere else. A private tutor might have made me proficient in French, in Algebra, even in Science. Of these subjects (partly, but only partly, because I had no natural bent for them) I knew next to nothing when I left Charterhouse. The main thing that I had learnt there, and have not yet forgotten, was a knack of understanding my fellow-creatures, of living in amity with them and not being rubbed the wrong way by their faults, and not rubbing them the wrong way with mine. I live in Italy nowadays, because I like the sun very much. But whenever I go to England my friends are really pleased to see me. I have not lost that good-humoured, give-and-take spirit which only the communal life of a public school could have given me. It is often complained that public schools tend to repress individuality in a child. Charterhouse in the eighteen-eighties did not at all tend that way—and doesn't, I am sure, now. Its traditions left plenty of latitude. I was a queer child. I didn't care a brass farthing for games. What I liked was Latin prose, Latin verse, and drawing caricatures. Nobody bothered me to play games. Boys and masters alike (Mr. Tod always especially) encouraged me to draw as many and as impudent caricatures as possible. I ought to have been very happy. But—oh, how I always longed to be grown-up! Boys are mostly not cursed with a strong instinct towards independence; nor men mostly, for the matter of that. I, alas, was. My lips duly said Adsum for me at the right moment, on the appointed spot. But my heart was always out of bounds. There was an old gentleman who used often to pass in front of the garden of Duckites, driving a phaeton slowly up the steep road. He wore a square-topped brown hat, he had an aquiline nose and a drooping white moustache and an air of command, and a groom behind him. I don't know who he was. But I knew that he could stay out as long as he liked, and would dress for dinner, and be dining while I sat in Banco, and be fast asleep when I was in Chapel next morning. I wished immensely that I were he. But now, after all, I am glad that I had to go on being myself. I rejoice that I was not able to skip even one of the years that were so good for me. And if ever I am born into a second incarnation ('Which Heaven forbid!' say my young readers) I hope I shall be sent back to my old school.

THE TOP HAT

(1940)

THE TOP HAT

(*1940.*)

'What is that?' the very young will ask; and their parents, ever quick to correct, will say to them, 'You mean, What *was* it?' For it is, of course, very definitely, a thing of the past; almost a museum piece. Indeed, some parents, those who are less than middle-aged, may not even have heard of it. I plead guilty to finding in the past a charm which the present lacks for me. I hasten to say, however, that this charm is slight in comparison with that which the future would have for me if I were youngish, for (I gather from many publicists) the future, the post-bellum period, is to be perfectly splendid: new men, new ideas, new policies, new cosmic outlooks, new hills and valleys, new Old Masters, new fathers and mothers, new wines, new Old Moore's Almanacs, new everything. But I, alas, shan't live to see much, or perhaps anything, of all that. And I fondly strain my time-dimmed eyes towards that backward horizon whereon stands the top hat, a black but shining old monument.

Just *how* old, I can't say. I do but know that it had been erected already in the later days of Charles James Fox. He wears a top hat in that fine portrait of him sitting in his garden, immensely corpulent, but still full of energy and animation, of benignity and genius. He wears it pushed cheerfully back from his brow, and it looks rather odd in relation to his knee-breeches: a queer blend of the new and the old century. It is a beaver hat, of course. The silken kind was a Victorian discovery. But I think that had I been in that garden when that portrait was in the making I should have been shocked that the sitter was not wearing a gold-laced tricorn; for even in those days I should not have been a great approver of current things. Fox himself, no doubt, was very proud of the new headgear. Perhaps he himself invented it? Had he not, a few years before, said in writing to a friend about the fall of the Bastille, 'How much the greatest thing it is in history! and how much the best!'? Strange that a hat that was to symbolise all that was most static and most reputable may have been designed by a man so dangerous!

I imagine that the Whigs, who in all things followed the beloved Charles like sheep, were soon enthusiastic wearers of the top hat, while the Tories looked on it with frigid horror and would none of it. But very soon, long before the dreadful Reform Bill, they themselves were wearing it, sullenly perhaps, but without protest. It had imposed itself upon them, with a mysterious and inexorable power that was somehow latent in it. It had ceased to be a sign of the times. It had become a natural phenomenon. It seemed to be even a part of the human body. Not merely did one hunt in it, as one still does: one fished, one skated, one played cricket in it. One wore it throughout debates in the Houses of Parliament, taking it off (with a wrench) only when one rose to orate, and resuming it (with a sigh of relief) as soon as ever one had said one's say. At routs and receptions, however great the crush, one carried it in one's hand all the time—and one must have been glad when, some time in the 'sixties, somebody invented the crush-hat, the gibus, which could be held under the arm, inobtrusively saving the situation. One kept it on one's head, even while eating luncheon in one's club. I don't think there are any clubs now where this custom survives. But it did survive in quite recent years at the 'In and Out', magically wafting any guest into a past age. Until quite lately, in theatres or opera houses, when you went out to smoke in the foyer, you always took your hat with you lest some evil thing should befall you. And when you paid an 'afternoon call' (a habit not then extinct) you would rather have died than not appear before your hostess hat in hand—and gloves there too. These things you presently placed upon the floor beside your chair, where she could still see them, symbols of good breeding and reassuring proclamations of the fact that you were only a visitor and hadn't come to abide with her forever.

On Sundays the top hat acquired an even sacred significance. When a family entered the family pew, the father, instead of kneeling down with his wife and children for some moments, merely sat forward and said his silent prayer into his hat. This always puzzled me. I did not grasp the underlying theory that a prayer offered through that medium was likely to be the more acceptable.

On Sundays at Oxford—I was going to use again the adverb 'recently', but though the time when I was a freshman seems to me only yesterday, it is now just half a century ago—there were still some undergraduates who honoured the day with top hats and frock-coats. And no undergraduate who, in defiance of proctorial regulations, dared to pay a flying visit to London, would have dared to do so without those urban insignia, though they invited detection on the way to the railway station. One bespoke a cab on the eve of the adventure, and on the morning of it one instructed the cabman to drive to the station very quickly; and on the platform, if one espied a donnish-looking man, one tried to look very old and irreproachable. A motor-car would have been a great convenience. But motor-cars were not yet. And the top hats which in later days they, as it were, bashed in, and the accompanying frock-coats which, so to speak, they ran over, were still vitally necessary to any young gentleman with any self-respect and respect for London.

Or, for that matter, to any decently modest young gentleman who didn't want to be stared at. In London even the crossing-sweepers mostly wore top hats. The 'old-clo'-men', those hoarsely vocal perambulants, went even further: they wore three, one rammed down on another, in token, I suppose, of big business. The policemen had indeed long ago taken to helmets—not, I am sure, of their own accord, but because some Home Secretary had thought they would look more frightening. There was only one other civilian body of men that did not follow the all-prevailing fashion: nearly all the actors wore billicocks. The comedians tended to wear brown ones, the tragedians black ones; and those tragedians who were Bohemian in their way of life were apt to prefer sombreros. The actor-manager attended rehearsals in a top hat; and a top hat could be worn also by any actor who had played leading parts in other theatres, and very careful was such an one to wear it, to the envy of less illustrious members of the cast. I always wished those others would combine to break loose and fly in the face of immemorial etiquette, boldly encylindered. But they never fulfilled my hope. Nowadays, I suppose, not even the most eminent and responsible of actors rehearses in anything but what (heaven knows why) is called a trilby. Alas, the Spirit of the Age is one that levels down, not up.

Bank-messengers, Westminster boys, the porter at either end of such places as the Albany or Palace Gardens Terrace, are faithful among the few. And there is of course the occasional, the spasmodic fidelity of men going to weddings or funerals, or (in peace time) to Ascot or the Eton and Harrow match. My heart is gladdened at sight of these? At the risk of seeming querulous, I protest that it isn't. The males of the Latin races are far less self-conscious than we, far more adaptable in the matter of costume. Carnival time in any French or Italian city is a very good time indeed. The revellers do revel in their fantastic attire, are urged up by it to the height of high spirits. But among my memories none is drearier than that of the Fancy Dress Balls which used to be given in Covent Garden Opera House. The women seemed happy enough, but the men—how woebegone! how deeply ashamed of themselves! The street acrobats of my childhood, in their spangles and pink tights, acquitted themselves quite gaily throughout their professional somersaults and other feats. But when they finished, when they fared along the pavements to their next pitch, what shuffling figures of embarrassment they did cut, to be sure! Not less awfully abashed by their own appearance are the gentlemen going their way to and from weddings or any other of those functions which involve what has become, quite obviously, fancy dress.

Perhaps after the present war the top hat will never reappear at any function whatsoever, even on the head of the eldest man. Perhaps it will be used as a flower-pot in the home, filled with earth and nourishing the bulb of a hyacinth or other domestic flower. I hope, in the goodness of my heart, the housemaid will not handle it untenderly, and will brush it the right way. For it is very sensitive. Its sensibility was ever one of its great charms. It alone among hats had a sort of soul. If one treated it well, one wasn't sure that it didn't love one. It wasn't as expressive as one's dog, yet it had an air of quiet devotion and humble comradeship. It had also, like one's cat, a great dignity of its own. And it was a creature of many moods. On dull cloudy days itself was dull, but when the sun was brightly shining, it became radiant. If it was out in a downpour of rain, without an umbrella, it suffered greatly: it was afflicted with a sort of black and blue rash, most distressing to behold, and had to be nursed back to health with tender and unremitting care. Nature herself was the best nurse, however, during the early stages of the malady. The patient was best left to grow quite dry by action of the air, before being ever so gently brushed with the softest of brushes. Gradually it became convalescent, and seemed to smile up at you while it was rubbed slowly with a piece of silk. And anon it was well enough to be ironed. When I was very young I used to have my hat ironed periodically at my hatter's, like other young men. Rather a fascinating process to watch!—the expert swiftness and sureness of it, the immense change wrought with a violent celerity that seemed dangerous and yet did no harm. But in later times I would not entrust my dumb friend to hireling hands howsoever trustworthy, and he almost spoke his gratitude to me when I purchased an iron of the kind required—or rather two irons, a wide one for shaft and crown, a narrow one for brim—and tentatively ironed him myself. At first my 'prentice hand was slow and faulty, and I never did quite master the art of swirling the curves of the iron with perfect symmetry around the crown. I must confess also that more than once, in the early days, I miscalculated the temperature of the iron and did grievous hurt to my friend—hurt so grievous that though he mutely assured me that it was no matter, and implored me not to abandon him, I had to secure a successor instantly.

But, as I look back across the gulf that lies between me and those Victorian and Edvardian years, I feel that I may justly claim to have deserved the affection my hats had for me. And I hope that my young readers will not scoff—though I fear they will—at the fulness with which that feeling was reciprocated by me.

FENESTRALIA

(1944)

FENESTRALIA

(*1944.*)

'The mother of Sisera looked out at a window, and cried through the lattice, Why is his chariot so long in coming? Why tarry the wheels of his chariot?'

A vivid scene, this, is it not? You *see* it, *hear* it; and you are moved by its dramatic irony, knowing what the mother does not know; knowing what Jael has done.

'And when Jehu came to Jezreel, Jezebel heard of it; and she painted her face and tired her head, and looked out at a window. And as Jehu entered in at the gate, she said, Had Imri peace that slew his master? And he lifted up his face to the window, and said, Who is on my side? who? And there looked out to him two or three eunuchs.'

Some dramatic irony here, too. Jezebel knows not, as do we, how imminent her doom is. But the irony is less poignant, forasmuch as Jezebel is not a sympathetic personage. We cannot, with the best will in the world, feel very sorry for her. Nevertheless, her words haunt us as do those of the mother of Sisera. Thanks, in some measure, to Coverdale, to Tyndale? No doubt. But also because her words were spoken, like those others, from a window.

Had either of those women been seated in a room, or walking in a garden, or looking across a wall, we should be far less impressed. People seen or things said indoors or out-of-doors have not the same arresting quality as things said or people seen half-indoors, half-out. There is much virtue in a window. It is to a human being as a frame is to a painting, as a proscenium to a play, as 'form' to literature. It strongly defines its content. It excludes all but what it encloses. It firmly rivets us. In fact, it's a magic casement.

I have set eyes on many great men, in my time, and have had the privilege of being acquainted with some of them (not of knowing them well, understanding them well, for to do that there must be some sort of greatness in oneself). And of all the great men whom I have merely seen the one who impressed me most was Degas. Some forty years ago I was passing, with a friend, through the Place Pigalle; and he, pointing up his stick to a very tall building, pointing up to an open window *au cinquième*—or was it *sixième*?—said, 'There's Degas.' And there, in the distance, were the head and shoulders of a grey-bearded man in a red béret, leaning across the sill. There Degas was, and behind him, in there, was his studio; and behind him, there in his old age, was his life-work; and with unageing eyes he was, I felt sure, taking notes of the 'values' and what not of the populous scene down below, regretting perhaps (for he had never cast his net wide) the absence of any ballet-dancers, or jockeys, or laundry-girls, or women sponging themselves in hip-baths; but deeply, but passionately observing. There he was, is, and will always be for me, framed.

Not perhaps a great, but certainly a gifted and remarkable man was Dr. Jowett, at first and last sight of whom, driving along the Broad in a landau, more than half a century ago, I, a freshman, experienced a mild thrill. How much less mild must have been the thrill vouchsafed to that party of visitors whom C. S. Calverley was showing over Balliol many years earlier! 'There', said Calverley, 'is the Jowler's window. And,' he added, having picked up a stone and hurled it at the window, 'there's the Jowler.' It is thus, and thus only, that a man is seen at his best—or, for that matter, a woman at hers. In Robert Browning's great galaxy of women none is so vivid to me as Riccardi's bride, and never have I passed Palazzo Riccardi without wondering whether 'The Statue and the Bust' would ever have been written had not Duke Ferdinand's first sight of that bride been framed in one of those windows, that window at which he was evermore content to see her, to leave her, day after day, as he rode by.

She, you will remember, when she was growing old, summoned to her presence Luca della Robbia and bade him mould a portrait of her at her habitual window, so that after her death she would still be there. And perhaps it was her example that in later times set the fashion of those *finte* which were until recent years so frequently to be seen on blank walls of Italian houses. These were not up to the standard of 'Robbia's craft so apt and strange'. They were indeed, if you will, rather vulgar. The average leaner-out was apt to be somewhat over-dressed in the complex mode of the eighteen-seventies, over-frilled, over-jewelled; and her blond tresses (for, of course, to suit the wistful taste of the Italians, she was always a *biondina*) were rather over-blond. The curtains of her window were of a very bright red or blue, and there was likely to be a very yellow canary in a cage beside her. And hers was a vapid simper as she leaned forth with one elbow on the cushioned sill, and one index finger posed upon her cheek. There was much to be said against her; yet one misses her, now that she's gone. She had the charm of windowhood.

I have often wondered that (barring the artless makers of those *finte*) so few painters have used that charm, woven that spell. Dante Gabriel Rossetti, one of those few, might, with his constant striving after 'intensity', have been expected to be a devotee of windows; but even he did but once avail himself of frame within frame. Once; and of all his portraits of women, haunting as these are by reason of what he saw in them, or transfused into them, assuredly the most haunting is that of the head and shoulders of a cottage girl at a small lattice window, a girl in a smock, drawing back a chequered curtain, looking out into the morning, and (one guesses) taking in the scent of the flowers in a small front-garden unseen by us. Behind her, unseen too, is her room, with such little belongings in it as are hers; and, just because it isn't visible, that room is a far better setting than those elaborate environments of wondrous fabrics, of mediæval bibelots and of exotic flowers in strange bowls or vases with which Rossetti, for the most part, endowed his models.

A great element in the charm of windows is that unless they are on the ground-floor and you flatten your nose against the panes you cannot see more than a very little, if anything at all, of what lies behind them. Your imagination has free play. Do you know those tiny little old half-length figures in waxwork at Hertford House?—those Spanish noblemen and noblewomen of the seventeenth century, each of them enshrined in a square box that is black outside and black inside and has one side made of glass to allow the inmate to look, sombrely, disdainfully out at us from what our fancy assures us is a great old august apartment in a worthy palace? I have often gazed at them, and never without an illusion of having been wafted back across three centuries into Madrid, or into Seville, and of seeing this and that great personage alive, haughtily in the flesh, at a great window. Henry James, roaming around the Boboli Gardens, some fifty years ago, paused and, gazing fixedly up at one of the windows of the vast stony palace, reflected that from *it* Medici after Medici had stood looking out. 'And the Medici were great people,' he mused, as he tells us in the essay that he presently wrote; and 'the ache of the historic spirit' in him was poignant. He would have experienced no such ache in that room on the ground-floor of Hertford House in which I so often stood before the windows of those minim waxworks. His historic sense would have blest and feasted.

Playwrights, like painters, have been chary of windows. Shakespeare, like Rossetti, used only one, once only, so far as I remember. He seems not to have realised that words spoken from a window are thereby as much the more effective as the person seen thereat. Stage-struck young ladies, by some queer instinct, are aware of this fact; hence the desire of all of them to commence as Juliet: the window will conceal incompetence. My most vivid memory of Mrs. Patrick Campbell is framed in the window of Mélisande. And this memory reminds me that Mélisande's was not the only window vouchsafed to us by Maurice Maeterlinck, and that of all his plays *Intérieur* was the most strangely moving and haunting. The foreground of the stage is a garden in the dusk of night. In the background there are the windows of a lighted room, in which, clearly visible, are the father and mother and sisters of a girl whose drowned body, as we know from the hushed and broken talk of the men and women in the garden, is being brought from the river. The mother and father and sister will soon know what is known to us. The action of the piece lasts no more than half-an-hour. But at the end of it one seems to have suffered a very long period of pity and awe.

Let me pass on to another play, in itself less remarkable than *Intérieur,* but far more famous and more popular. Its author is nameless, its action is crudely barbarous, its dialogue is but shrill incoherent gibberish. Yet it has for all of us, whenever we come across it, a perennial fascination. How can we account for that? Easily enough. The whole drama is enacted in a window-frame, the frame of the one and only window in Punch's strange old portable house.

Politicians, please note. The gift of oratory has been conferred on few of you; nor are many of you able to express yourselves fluently, accurately, and without grievous triteness. Think how much less restive your audiences would be if you spoke to them through a window! My temperament was conservative even in my youth. My mind, moreover, was ossified years ago. I abominate all alterations. But for your sakes I do hope you will insist that St. Stephen's new Chamber shall have a small inner structure, simple or ornate, with a window through which all speeches shall be delivered. Let me also commend to you a similar device on the platforms of Town Halls. Even that baker's dozen of you who *can* speak with the tongue of men and angels, and can hold their constituents or their fellow-Members spellbound, would find their triumphs enhanced by my scheme. I suppose that the greatest English orator in the nineteenth century was Mr. Gladstone; and I take it to have been the peak of his achievements in the spoken word that on a bitterly cold afternoon, and on Blackheath Common, at the time of the Bulgarian Atrocities, he dominated and swayed for one hour and a half a gathering of not less than six thousand persons, most of whom had violently booed him at the outset of his speech. There, indeed, was a man who could dispense with windows. Yet, in later years, in the Midlothian phase of his career, he made frequent use of them. And I feel sure his greatest effects were made in those successive railway stations where, to serried throngs, he spoke burning words from the window of a railway-carriage, on his way northward or southward. I can see that ivory face and that silvery hair; and those dark flashing eyes looking forth. Would that I had been there to hear the organ-music of the voice!

Gladstone's great rival and antithesis was no man for mobs, and excelled only in the Chamber. But he did have one great success in presence of a multitude. I refer to the one and only occasion on which he spoke from a window. I wish I had been old enough to be in the crowd down to which, from a frame on the first floor of 10 Downing Street, he made his pronouncement about Peace with Honour. I should like also, of course, to have heard him in parliamentary debate. I was once told by an old gentleman who had sat on the back benches, as a Conservative member, when Mr. Disraeli was Leader of the House, that sphinx-like though the face was to all beholders the great debater's back was very expressive—the movements of the shoulders, of the elbows and the hips vividly illustrating his words. But even in repose a back, if it be of the right kind, can be eloquent—such a back as Goethe's, for example. Do you know that sketch which Johann Tischbein made in one of the bedrooms of a Roman inn, while Goethe was leaning out of the window and looking down to the street below? It is a graceful, a forceful, and a noble back that we see there in that bedroom. Had Napoleon been there to see it, he would have murmured, as you know he did when he saw Goethe face to face at Weimar in later years, 'Voilà un homme!' It is moreover the back of a man rapt in contemplation, rapt in the joy of being, at last, in the city of his dreams; a man avidly observing, learning, storing up. He is wearing slippers, he has not yet put on his waistcoat nor buttoned his breeches at the knees. His toilet can wait. His passionate curiosity cannot. It is as intimate, as significant a portrait as ever was made of one man by another.

I like to think that it may have been made on Goethe's very first morning in Rome, and that he had arrived overnight. In visiting a city that you have never yet seen it is well to arrive at night, for sake of the peculiar excitement of next morning's awakening to it—the queer deep thrill of your prospection into whatever street or square underlies your window, presaging all else that will be seen later. A square is preferable to a street; a populous old spacious square, set with statues and animated by fountains; somewhere in Italy, for choice. Such a square is a good starting-point for your future rovings; and to it from them you will always return with a feeling of affection, and will spend much time at that window of yours, fondly. But I beg your pardon for dogmatising about you. When I said *you,* I meant *I.* You perhaps are an ardent sight-seer, a scrupulous examiner of aisles and sacristies and side-chapels, an indefatigable turner-in at turnstiles of museums and picture-galleries and the like. I'm an alfrescoist. The life of the city, and the architectural background against which that life is lived, suffice my soul while I rove around, or merely lean forth from the window that is, for the time being, mine. Merely? I take back that word. One is more observant from one's coign of vantage up there, and all that is to be seen stands out more clearly, and one's mind is more sensitive, than when one pads the hoof down there.

'The last time I saw Paris'—otherwise than from the ceinture railway—abides with me more vividly and delightfully than any of the previous times. Yet I saw but one aspect of the city's life. You know the huge grey façade of the Gare du Nord, and may have noted that it is adorned (or at any rate weighted) with rows of proportionately huge statues, one on each side of every window, symbolising the Continents, and the principal French provinces and cities, and Liberty, I think, and Justice, and many other things of national or universal import. But you may not be aware that all the windows on the first floor are those of an hotel, an hotel that occupies this one floor only, and consists of twelve vast bedrooms (each with a small anteroom and a bathroom), and nothing else. Behind the bedrooms runs a corridor whose opposite side has windows through which you see, far down, the many platforms of the station and the steam of arriving and departing trains. These windows are of thick double glass. The corridor is a quiet one. Little locomotives are seen and not heard. But the bedrooms are the great point. They seem to have been built for giants and giantesses, so vast are their ancient wardrobes, dressing-tables, and beds; and each of their two windows is in proportion to the stone figure that stands on either side of it, planting a colossal foot upon the sill. If I remember rightly, it was from between the ankle of a masculine Africa and of a feminine Marseilles that I looked forth early on my first morning, and saw a torrent of innumerable young human backs, flooding across the square beneath and along the straight wide Rue Lafayette beyond. The fulness and swiftness of it made me gasp—and kept me gasping, while in the station behind me, incessantly, for more than an hour and a half, trainload after trainload of young men and women from the banlieue was disgorged into the capital. The maidens outnumbered the youths by about three or four to one, it seemed to me; and yet they were one maiden, so identically alike were they in their cloche hats and knee-deep skirts and flesh-coloured stockings, and in virtue of that erectly tripping gait which Paris teaches while London inculcates an unsteady slouch. One maiden, yet hundreds and thousands of maidens, each with a soul of her own, and a home of her own, and earning her own wages. Bewildering! Having seen that sight, I needed no other. During the three or four days of my sojourn I didn't bother to go anywhere, except for meals in a little restaurant hard by, famous for its oysters and its bouillabaisse. I spent my time in reading newspapers and books, and in looking forward to the early morrow's renewal of the incalculable torrent.

From some windows one can gaze and be rapt at any hour of the day, even though no human being is to be seen from them. From any window, for instance, that looks out on to the sea. For many years I lived in a little house that looks down to what a great poet, reared beside Northumbrian breakers, rudely called 'the tideless dolorous midland sea'. It has a tide really (though not perhaps a very great one), and its aspect is constantly changing, and I was never tired of watching it and its moods. I remember, too, with affection, the little bedroom in an old farm-house at Pagham, where I abode for some weeks of the autumn after the last war. There were a few stairs up to the bedroom, but the window was so placed that its sill was no more than five feet or so above the level of the ground. Outside there was nothing to be seen but a large field of ripening barley. The sea was quite near, but invisible. One was all alone with the barley, which grew in a friendly eager manner right up against the wall of the farm-house, inviting one to lean down and touch its ears.

Let not such memories imply any disparagement of quite ordinary windows—street windows, with recurrent glimpses of neighbours opposite. I am glad that from the windows of my nursery in a Victorian cul-de-sac I knew by sight various other children, and their nurses, and their parents. I had no great desire to know them outside their frames. I think I had a shrewd suspicion that they were not really so interesting and so exciting as my fancy made them. In my adolescence no neighbours were to be seen. Nevertheless, I was fond of my bedroom window, from which I could gaze in a moralising manner over the multitude of tombstones in what had been throughout the eighteenth century the burial-ground of St. George's, Hanover Square; and I was still fonder of my sitting-room window, from which I could watch, year after year, the budding of the leaves in Hyde Park, and their prime, and their decline and fall. Trees are of course the best thing Nature has to show us; and in London one values them far more than one does elsewhere. I missed them sorely when, in later years, I lived in a street again. The faces at the windows over the way were unchanging, were unaffected by the sequence of the seasons. Also, alas, my talent for weaving fancies was not what it once had been. Still, I was a frequent looker-forth—especially on Thursdays. I had become a professional writer. I wrote a weekly article for *The Saturday Review;* and Thursday was the day on which I did it; and the doing was never so easy as I sometimes hoped it might be: I had never, poor wretch, acquired one scrap of professional facility. I often doubted whether I had in my mind enough to fill the two columns that were expected of me. I sometimes found that I had got ahead of my argument, or even that I was flatly contradicting something that I had said at the outset, or that my meaning was obscure even to myself. At such crises I would rise from my desk and take, as it were, refuge at the window, with brows knitted, and chin tightly clasped between finger and thumb. I would envy the hansom cabmen as they flashed by below me. I would envy some old lady leading a dog on a leash. I would envy her dog.

'And if it was thus, thus in the prime of me,' need I say that the composition of what you have just been reading or skipping was not done without much recourse to a window?

T. FENNING DODWORTH

(1922)

T. FENNING DODWORTH

(1922.)

This name is seldom, if ever, on the lips of the man in the street. But it is a name highly esteemed by men whose good opinion is most worth having. When the idols of our market-place shall have been jerked from their pedestals by irreverent Time, Fenning Dodworth will not be utterly forgotten. His name will crop up *passim,* and honourably, in the pages of whatever Grevilles and Creeveys we have had among us during the past thirty years.—'Met Fenning Dodworth in Pall Mall this morning. He told me he had it on the best authority that St. John Brodrick would not be put up to speak on the Second Reading.'—'Heard an amusing and characteristic *mot* of Fenning Dodworth's. He was dining with some other men at E. Beckett's one night last week, when the conversation turned on Winston's speech at Oldham. Beckett said, "Whatever Winston's faults may be, he has genius." "That," said Dodworth, in the silence that ensued, "is a proposition on which I should like to meditate before endorsing it." Collapse of Beckett!'—'Sat next to Dodworth at the Cordwainers' dinner. He said that he did not at all like the look of things in the Far East. Later in the evening I asked him point-blank whether the phrase "A Government of Pecksniffs", which has been going the rounds, had been coined by him. "It may have been," he said drily. Characteristic!'

Dodworth's wit is undeniable. It is not, certainly, of the kind that I like best and rate highest—the kind that pierces without leaving a wound. Dodworth's shafts are barbed, and, though it were too much to say that they are poisoned, assuredly they have been dipped in very caustic acids. And he has not humour. At least, if he has, he uses it sparingly, and never at all in my presence. But humour, delightful though it is for current purposes, lacks durability. There are fashions in humour, and they are always changing. Wit, on the other hand, being a hard and clean-cut thing, is always as good as new. Dodworth's gems, set in the golden tissue of private journals given to the world, will have lost nothing of their flash. And among readers of those journals there will be a great desire to know what Dodworth himself was like. Keepers of journals are so apt to omit that sort of thing. What faces, complexions, girths, heights, gaits, voices, gestures, tricks of manner, shirt-studs, preferences in food and wine, had the more or less eminent men who were forever pouring into the diarist's ear their hopeful or fearful conjectures about to-morrow night's Division? The diarist knew, and had therefore no need to tell himself. But *we* don't know, and we want to know. That Division was a turning-point in the world's history? No doubt. Those more or less eminent men are dust? Alas, yes. But they were flesh and blood to the diarist, and he could have made them so to us, too. It may be that the diarists of our own day have held in mind the omissions of their forerunners, and make a point of telling themselves just the things that are a matter of course to them. But it may be otherwise. So I insert here, for posterity, a note or two on the surface of Fenning

Dodworth—who, quite apart from his wit, seems to me one of the most remarkable, the strongest and, in a way, most successful men of our time.

Dignity, a Roman dignity, is the keynote of his appearance. This is undoubtedly one of the causes of his success. Is it also, I sometimes ask myself, partly a result of his success? But no. Twenty years ago (when first I made his acquaintance) he was as impressive as he is, at the age of sixty, now. Moreover, had his mind any knack to remould his body, surely he would be taller. He remains very far below the middle height. But he carries his head high, thus envisaging the more easily the ruck of common objects, and making on such of those objects as are animate the kind of effect which his unaided stature might preclude. One of his eyebrows is slightly raised; the other is slightly lowered, to hold in position a black-rimmed single eyeglass. His nose is magnificently Roman. His lips are small, firm, admirably chiselled, and every word that falls from them is very precisely articulated. His chin is very strong, and his chest (in proportion to his height) deep. He has the neatest of hands and feet. Draped in a toga, and without his monocle, he might pass for a statuette of Seneca. But he prefers and affects a more recent style of costume—the style, somewhat, of the Victorian statesmen who flourished in his youth: a frock-coat and a rather large top-hat, a collar well-open at the throat, and round it a riband of black silk tied in a loose bow. He is a good judge (and, I take it, the sole survivor among judges) of sherry. Nor is this the only way in which he imparts agreeably the flavour of a past age. In Thackeray, in Trollope, in the old volumes of *Punch*, you will have found a wealth of testimony to the fact that persons of high importance, meeting persons of slight importance, often did not shake hands, but offered a finger or two to be shaken. Incredible, nevertheless? Then perhaps you will not believe me when I say that I have been offered two fingers by Dodworth. Indignantly you ask whether I shook them. I avoid your eye, I evade your question, I do but say that I am very susceptible to—well, to greatness.

The proof, for me, of Dodworth's greatness is in what he has achieved. He has made so much out of so little. Many men have been ten times more successful (in the coarse sense of that word) without winning a tithe of what he has won. It is often said that nothing succeeds like success. Dodworth's career offers a corrective of such cynicism—or would do so if his case were a common one. I admit that to have excelled in some undertaking is not always needed for the making of a great prestige. Dukes and princes are not without honour even if they have done nothing—or even if they shall have tried to do something and failed. Dodworth was not born exempt from the advisability of doing something. '*b.* 12. Feb. 1860, *o.s.* of J. Dodworth and Rachel, *e.d.* of W. K. Fenning, of Norwich.' Thus does he speak, in *Who's Who*, of his origin; and as he is (albeit less a toady than any man I know) one of the most finished snobs I have ever met, his reticence tells much. Old Mr. Dodworth was of some town so mean that it is not mentionable. And what did he do there? What, for that matter, did old Mr. Fenning do at Norwich? Something dreadful, you may be sure, from the social standpoint. What school was the young Dodworth sent to? Obviously to some school, else we should find '*Educ:* privately.' There is no mention of any school. The boy went to some school that is unmentionable. But it may be surmised that he did well there, for we do find '*Educ:* Won open scholarship at Queens Coll., Oxford, 1879.' A presage, this, of coarse successes. But mark the sequel! 'Second Class in Classical Mods., 1881; Third Class, Lit. Hum., 1883. Treasurer of Union, 1882.' He was thrice a candidate for the Presidency of the Union; and I happen to have met in later years two of his successful opponents, both of them men rather prominent in public life to-day. One of them told me that Dodworth's speeches were the wittiest ever heard in the Union 'or, I do believe, anywhere else'; the other described them as the most closely reasoned. And neither of these men spoke of Fenning Dodworth as one who had not lived up to his early promise. They seemed to pride themselves, rather, on having always foreseen his ascendancy.

Men prominent in public life are mostly hard to converse with. They lack small-talk, and at the same time one doesn't like to confront them with their own great themes. I have found that the best way to put them at their ease, to make them expand and glow, is to mention Fenning Dodworth. They are all, from their various standpoints, of one mind about him. Judges think he would have been an ornament to the Bench, statesmen wish he were in the Cabinet, diplomatists wish he were one of them, and wish he could be at Tokyo or Pekin or wherever at the moment his grasp of things in the Far East and his unfailing dislike of the look of them would be most obviously invaluable. And all these gods console themselves with anecdotes of his wit—some mordant thing he said years ago, some equally mordant thing he said last week. 'I remember,' a Judge will tell you, 'one night at mess on the Northern Circuit, somebody said "I call Bosanquet a very strong man in Nisi Prius." Dodworth looked at him in that queer dry way of his, and said "Ah! I should hardly go so far as that."' The judge will then throw himself back in his chair and alarm you with symptoms of choking. If you ask him why Dodworth did not remain at the Bar, the answer will be that he got so few briefs: 'He was the best all-round Junior I ever heard, but he wasn't a man for the jury: you can't saw a plank of wood with a razor. Pity he didn't practise in Chancery! But I suppose he was right to devote himself to politics. He's had more scope there.'

He has not, certainly, been cramped. For him there has been no durance within the four walls of the House of Commons. He contested (I quote again his narrative in *Who's Who*) 'East Grinstead, 1888; Dulwich, 1890; Skipton, 1891; Cannock, 1893; Haggerston, 1897; Pontypool, 1898; Peebles, 1900.' He escaped, every time, the evils of election. (And his good angel stood not less close to him on the three occasions when he offered himself as candidate for the London County Council.) Voters, like jurors, would not rise to him. At length it was borne in even on the leaders of his party that they must after all be content to rely on his pen rather than on his tongue. 'Has been,' he says in *Who's Who*, 'for many years a contributor to the leading reviews.' That is so. Those reviews are not edited by the vulgar. Dodworth's MSS. have always been printed. I used to read articles by him when I was yet a schoolboy, and to wonder whether the Liberal Party would ever again hold up its hideous head. I remember one entitled 'The Franchise Bill—And After', and another entitled 'The

Home Rule Peril–And After'. Both seemed to me splendid, partly perhaps because of their titles. Dodworth was, I believe, the first publicist to use that magical affix, that somehow statesmanlike, mysterious, intriguing formula, '–And After'. In later years I began to think him narrow in his views. I became a prey to that sentimentalism from which in one's schooldays one is immune, and ceased to regard the ideas of the Liberal Party as perverse. Dodworth as a political thinker seemed to me lacking in generosity, lacking even (despite his invariable '–And After') in foresight. But the older I grew, and the less capable of his doctrine, the more surely did I appreciate his command of literary form. Losing the taste which undergraduates have for conceits and florid graces, I rendered justice to the sombre astringency of Dodworth's prose. Whatever his theme, whatever the Liberal Party was in office proposing, or in opposition opposing, his article was substantially the same as every other article he had written; but, like some masterpiece in music, it never palled. With perfect sobriety and fairness he would state the arguments on which the Liberal spokesmen had been basing their case; he would make these *seem* quite unanswerable; but then, suddenly, like a panther crouching to spring, he would pause, he would begin a new paragraph: What are the facts? The panther had sprung. It was always a great moment. I usually skipped the forthcoming facts and went on to the point where Dodworth worked back to first principles and historic parallels and (best of all) quotations from the mighty dead. He was always very adept in what may be called the suspensive method of quotation. 'It was written long ago, by one who saw further and grasped more firmly than is given to most men to see and to grasp, that "the fate of nations is in the conscience of their rulers." It is for us to ask ourselves whether, in saying this, Mr. Burke was right.' Or, 'In a speech delivered in the Guildhall at a time when Europe stood in the shadow of great events, a First Minister of the Crown, as to whom not a few of us are agreed in wishing that he were alive to-day, said that the art of government lay in the construction of safeguards. Mr. Disraeli never spoke a truer word.' But presently, with a swoop from the past to the present, and from the general to the particular, the scholar would be merged in the panther, and the Liberal Party be mauled so frightfully that at last even the panther seemed to recoil in pity for 'a Party once great' and to wonder if some excuse could not be found for it. The excuse, the last sentence of Dodworth's article, was usually *Quos deus vult perdere prius dementat;* but sometimes, more simply and poignantly, *Quos deus vult.*

Fifteen years ago it seemed to the leaders of his Party and to the veiled prophets in their Central Office, that such a voice as his, if it were heard daily by a vast public, would be proportionately more potent than in its monthly addresses to the few. There was an old-established daily newspaper whose proprietor had just died, and his estate not yet been wound up. And there was, on one of the back benches of the Party, a stout, silent man, middle-aged, very affluent, a Mister. Some word in season, some word in the ear, was spoken to this man, on a moonless night, by one of the veiled prophets. That old-established newspaper was acquired. Dodworth was installed in the editorial chair, gave the keynote to the staff, and wrote every night a leading article with his own incisive pen. But 'you cannot,' as the Judge said, 'saw a plank of wood with a razor.' To uneducated readers the almost-daily-recurring phrase *Quos deus vult* had no meaning. Half-educated readers thought it meant 'The Lord watch between thee and me when we are absent one from another.' The circulation fell by leaps and bounds. Advertisers withdrew their advertisements. Within six months (for the proprietor was now a Sir, and oafishly did not want to become something better) that old-established newspaper ceased utterly to be. 'This,' I thought, 'really *is* a setback for Dodworth.' I was far from right. The setback was rather for myself. I received no payment for three or four of the book-reviews that I had contributed, and I paid two guineas for my share of the dinner offered to Dodworth at the Savoy Hotel, and five guineas towards a portrait of him 'in oils' by one of the oldest and worst of Royal Academicians. This portrait was presented to him after dinner by our chairman (the Prime Minister of that time) in a speech that would have been cloying if it had been more fluent. Dodworth bandied no compliments. This was a private occasion, and he lived up to his reputation of being privately as caustic about his friends as he was publicly about his foes. He 'twitted' his friend the Prime Minister with one thing and another, reducing that statesman and the whole company to paroxysms of appreciation. . . . 'Our chairman has said that he will continue to do what in him lies to help the cause that we all have at heart (hear, hear). Well, wherever there is a cause there is also an effect (laughter). I hope that the effect in this instance will be of the kind that we all desiderate (much laughter). I do not say that it will be, I only say I hope it will be (hysterics).' I wish I could recall more of what Dodworth said. Every one agreed that he was in his best vein and had never been more pungent.

Two or three years later I attended another banquet at which he was the guest of the evening—a banquet at the Hotel Cecil, offered by the Playgoers' Club. He had written a three-act comedy: 'THE ANTAGONISTS—A Satire on Certain Aspects of Political Life'. This had been instantly snapped up, and soon produced, with a very strong cast, by Sir George Alexander. All the leaders of both parties in both Houses were present on the first night, and many of them (rashly, so weak were they with laughter) were present also on the second, third and fourth nights, and would probably have been present on other nights, too; but (such was the absenteeism of the vulgar) there were no other nights. Dodworth had again not sawn the plank. But it was clear to me, a week later, on the Sunday evening fixed—some time previously—for the banquet, that the edge of his razor was quite unblunted. In responding to the speech of the President (who had said nothing to imply that the play was not still running), Dodworth taunted us, very tartly, with our failure to arrest the decay of dramatic art by elevating the taste of the public. Had he been less witty, he might rather have spoilt our evening, so deep did he plant in us a sense of our failure. His own peculiar strength was never better attested than when, later in the evening, Alexander rose and announced with pride that he had that morning secured from his friend Fenning Dodworth the promise to write another comedy for the St. James's Theatre.

As this was never performed, I am quite sure it was never written. And I think the cause of the unfulfilment is to be found in the history of our time. Politics had now become too tense and terrible for the lighter use of Dodworth's pen. After the death of Sir Henry Campbell-Bannerman 'a Party once great' cast off what old remnants of decency had clung to it. Mr. Lloyd George composed a Budget. The Lords rejected it. Mr. Asquith introduced the Parliament Bill. Those were stirring times; and during them, as it seemed to me, Dodworth was greater, aye! and happier, than he had ever been. Constitutional points and precedents had always lain very near to his heart. In them he had always both publicly and privately abounded. His dislike of the look of things in the Far East had never been more than skin-deep. Such themes as the Reform Bill of 1832 had ever touched him to far finer issues. The fiscal problems raised by Mr. Chamberlain, strongly though he had backed Mr. Chamberlain's solution of them, had left in abeyance what was best in him. The desirability of enriching some rich manufacturers cannot be expressed in the grand manner. Mr. Asquith's desire to limit the Lords' veto was a worthy theme. Month followed month. I soon lost count of Dodworth's articles. 'The Assault on the Constitution–And After', 'The Betrayal–And After', 'The End of All Things–And After', are the only three that I recall. Enough that he was at his best in all of them, and ended every one of them with the inference that Mr. Asquith (one of his staunchest though most reluctant admirers) was mad.

I had the good fortune to meet him constantly in those days of crisis. I hardly know how this was. I did not seek him out. It seemed simply that he had become ubiquitous. Maybe his zest had multiplied him by 100 or so, enabling him to be in as many places at once. He looked younger. He talked more quickly than was his wont, though with an elocution as impeccable as ever. He had none of those austere, prim silences for which he was so feared. He was a bard. His command of the nobler, the statesmanlike kind of slang, and his unction in the use of it, had never been so mesmeric. 'If the Sovereign sent for the P.M. and said "I shall do nothing till the case arises," what could the P.M. say? Nothing. On the other hand, if the P.M. sought audience to-morrow *with a view to a contingent assurance,* and the Sovereign said "That's all very well, but what d'you hypothecate?" and the P.M. simply referred him back to what Mr. G. said when The Buffalo was threatening to throw out the Franchise of '85–*then* what? The Sovereign would be in a damned ticklish position. And the only way out of it', etc. Little wonder that agéd ears played truant at his tales, and younger hearings were quite ravishéd, so sweet and voluble was his discourse.

Alas, the Sovereign did not slip through whatever loop-hole it was that Dodworth descried. The P.M. did not climb down. The Buffalo did not rise from the grave. Lord L. sold the pass. The backwoodsmen went back to the backwoods. Dodworth was left sitting among the ruins of the Constitution. But the position suited him. He was still in his element, and great. It was at the outbreak of the War that I feared there might be no more of him. And there was, indeed, less. No longer young, he did not acquire more than a smattering of the military idiom, nor any complete grasp of strategy. But he was ever in close touch with the War Office and with G.H.Q., and was still fairly oracular. Several times in the last year of the conflict, he visited (with temporary rank of Lieutenant-Colonel) certain sectors of the Western Front and made speeches to the men in the trenches, declaring himself well-satisfied with their *morale,* and being very caustic about the enemy; but it may be doubted whether he, whose spell had never worked on the man in the street, was fully relished by the men in the trenches. *Non omni omnia.* Colonel Dodworth was formed for successes of the more exquisite kind. I think the Ministry of Information erred in supposing that his article, 'Pax Britannica—And After', would be of immense use all the world over. But the error was a generous one. The article was translated into thirty-seven foreign languages and fifty-eight foreign dialects. Twelve million copies of it were printed on hand-woven paper, and these were despatched in a series of special trains to a southern port. The Admiralty, at the last moment, could not supply transport for them, and the local authorities complained of them that they blocked the dock. The matter was referred to the Ministry of Reconstruction, which purchased a wheat-field twenty miles inland and erected on it a large shed of concrete and steel for the reception of Dodworth's pamphlets, pending distribution. This shed was nearly finished at the moment when the Armistice was signed, and it was finished soon after. Whether the pamphlets are in it, or just where they are, I do not know. Blame whom you will. I care not. Dodworth had even in the War another of his exquisite successes.

Yet I am glad for him that we have Peace. At first I was afraid it might be bad for him. We had been promised a new world; and to that, though he had come so well through the War, I feared he would not be able to adjust himself. The new world was to be, in many respects, rather dreadful—a benign cataclysm, but still a cataclysm, and Dodworth perhaps not to be found in any of his favourite chairs when the crystal waters subsided and the smiling land was revealed. We may have it yet. But the danger seems to be less imminent. A few days ago I met Dodworth in Bird-Cage Walk, and said to him something about it seeming likely that moderate counsels would prevail among the Labour men. 'Ah,' he said in that queer dry way of his, 'it's their moderate intelligence that's the danger.' He said it instantly (and it was obviously not a thing he could have prepared). And the very fact that he was able to jest once more was a heartening proof for me of his belief that the worst was past. Another good sign was that he had resumed his top-hat. During the last eighteen months of the War he had worn a thing of soft black felt, which I took to be a symbol of inward pessimism; and he had gone on wearing this long after the treaty of Peace was signed—a retention which seemed to me equally sinister, as a silent manifesto of unfaith in the future of our body politic. But now he was crowned once more with a cylinder from his old Victorian block. And a further good sign was that he was on his way to the House. In the old days, he had been wont to occupy, whenever an important debate was afoot, one or another of those nice seats near the Serjeant-at-Arms. In the course of the War he had ceased from such attendance. He had become very bitter against 'the politicians' and especially 'the lawyer politicians'. But I suspect that what revolted him even more was the sight of the new, the 'business' types on the Treasury Bench—the bullet-headed men in reefer-jackets, rising to tell the House what they were 'out for' and what they were 'up against', and why they had 'pushed' this and 'turned down' that, and forgetting to address the Chair. Dodworth's return to St. Stephen's implied for me the obsolescence of such men. I asked him what he thought, from a tactical standpoint, of the line recently taken by the Independent Liberals. 'I am afraid,' he said, 'there is not much hope for these Adullamites without a Cave.' This phrase he may not have coined on the spur of the movement. But, even so, how extraordinarily good! It's wicked, it's unjust, it hurts, but—it seems to me even more delicious than his description of Gladstone in '86 as 'a Moses without a Pisgah'. I think he was pleased, in his queer dry way, by my delight, for he said he would send me a copy of his forthcoming book—a selection from the political articles written by him since his earliest days. He had not, he said (quoting, I think, from his preface), intended to resuscitate these ephemeræ. The idea was not his but ——'s (he named the head of an historic firm of publishers). The book will be out next month, and will include that most recent of his articles, 'A Short Shrift for Sinn Fein—And After'. It will be 'remaindered', of course, in a year or so, but will meanwhile have taken an honoured place in every eminent man's library. By the way, I had feared that Mr. Lloyd George, with his Celtic rather than classic mind, made a break in the long line of Prime Ministers who have rated Dodworth highly. I am glad to hear that at a dinner held somewhere the night before last he impulsively rose and proposed Dodworth's health, recalling that when he himself was a bare-legged, wild-eyed, dreamy little lad on the Welsh mountains he read every word of Fenning Dodworth's earlier articles as they came out, and had never forgotten them (applause). Since those days he had met Dodworth many a time in the valley and got some resounding whacks (laughter). But he always felt, and more than ever he felt to-night, that Dodworth and he were destined to walk hand in hand on the heights, misty though those heights might be now, and hail together the glory of the sunrise that, sooner or later, had got to come (prolonged applause). My informant tells me that of all the eyes around the table Dodworth's alone were dry, and maintains that in returning thanks he ought not to have been pungent. I disagree. I want no signs of weakness in dear old Dodworth.

Dear old Dodworth? Well, no–and yet *yes*, too. I don't like him, perhaps; but there is no man whom I so delight to see, to watch, and to think of. I hope he will not predecease me. Of one thing I am sure: he will die game, and his last words will be '–And After?' and will be spoken pungently. And of another thing I am sure; the eminent men of all kinds will sign a petition about him to the Dean of Westminster. But there is a tradition of Philistinism in that Deanery. The voices of the eminent fall on deaf ears there, and only the roar of the man in the street is heard. Dodworth will, characteristically, not have the coarse success of lying in our Abbey. His monument will be found–piecemeal, indeed, but great, but glittering–in the diaries which I mentioned at the outset of this little essay in his honour.

MAY 15-18, 1964

A NOTE ON THE TYPE

The text of this book is set in Caledonia, a Linotype face designed by W. A. Dwiggins, the man responsible for so much that is good in contemporary book design and typography. Caledonia belongs to the family of printing types called "modern face" by printers – a term used to mark the change in style of type-letters that occurred about 1800. It has all the hard-working feet-on-the-ground qualities of the Scotch Modern face plus the liveliness and grace that is integral in every Dwiggins "product" whether it be a simple catalogue cover or an almost human puppet.

The book was composed, printed, and bound by The Plimpton Press, Norwood, Massachusetts.